Contents

Every section includes practice materials for these 10 topics:

Unit 1: Greetings and Useful Phrases

Unit 2: Introductions

Unit 3: Numbers, Dates, Time, and Money (I)

Unit 4: Numbers, Dates, Time, and Money (II)

Unit 5: Locating Persons, Places, and Things

Unit 6: Biographical Information (I)

Unit 7: Biographical Information (II)

Unit 8: Getting Around Beijing (I)

Unit 9: Getting Around Beijing (II)

Unit 10: Weather

Additional Practice Materials in Printable PDF Format: See the Disc!

How to Use These Materials

Basic Mandarin Chinese—Speaking & Listening Practice Book contains extensive drills and exercises for each unit of the textbook *Basic Mandarin Chinese—Speaking & Listening*. The purpose of this workbook is to offer learners various kinds of practice activities for both in- and out-of-class use, so as to enable learners to reinforce and "activize" their learning of the new vocabulary and grammar introduced in the textbook.

New Vocabulary and Grammar Summaries

The first section of the *Practice Book* consists of a one-page list of new vocabulary and grammar in each *Basic Mandarin Chinese—Speaking & Listening* lesson, from Unit 1, Part 1 through Unit 10, Part 4.

The lists are divided into a section on "Vocabulary" and a section on "Grammar." In the vocabulary section, each new vocabulary item introduced in the corresponding lesson of the textbook is listed in alphabetical order of the Pinyin with English translation and indication of word class (any Additional Vocabulary is not included). In the grammar section, each new grammar pattern introduced in that part of the textbook is listed, also in alphabetical order, in most cases with one or more examples in Pinyin and English translation.

- We believe these lists of new vocabulary and grammar will be useful for all learners for review purposes. However, learners should ideally not learn new vocabulary or grammar from these lists; instead, they should always try to learn new vocabulary and grammar in the context of the Basic Conversations and Build Ups in the textbook.

- Those learners who are using the *Practice Book* to supplement other textbooks and who do not have access to the textbook for *Basic Mandarin Chinese—Speaking & Listening*, will want to pay special attention to these lists, since the various drills and exercises in this book assume thorough familiarity with all this material.

The next two sections consist of **drills**. Don't underestimate the value of drills as enabling mechanisms that help you, the learner, to attain the ultimate goal of communicative competency. The drills are useful for improving your pronunciation, developing your fluency, and increasing your confidence in speaking Chinese. Although it's true that some of the drills in this workbook are of necessity fairly mechanical, others are more realistic and communicative, in some cases even incorporating a certain amount of cultural material.

- The drills are best done out of class in self-study mode, either in a language learning laboratory or, working with a computer or your audio player, in some other place of your choosing. If you're learning Chinese in a classroom setting, doing the drills out of class also frees up valuable time with the instructor so that you can focus on those kinds of interactive learning activities for which the instructor's guidance and active participation are essential.

- You should work with the recordings on the accompanying disc as actively as possible, speaking loudly and always thinking of the meaning of what you are hearing and saying.

- If you're learning Chinese on your own, the drills will be especially important for you and, working with the accompanying audio disc, you should try to go through each one several times. In addition, it will be to your benefit to seek out a native-speaking tutor or mentor who can work with you one or two hours a week for additional practice and to answer questions.

BASIC
MANDARIN
CHINESE

SPEAKING & LISTENING

PRACTICE BOOK

CORNELIUS C. KUBLER & YANG WANG

TUTTLE Publishing

Tokyo | Rutland, Vermont | Singapore

ABOUT TUTTLE
"Books to Span the East and West"

Our core mission at Tuttle Publishing is to create books which bring people together one page at a time. Tuttle was founded in 1832 in the small New England town of Rutland, Vermont (USA). Our fundamental values remain as strong today as they were then—to publish best-in-class books informing the English-speaking world about the countries and peoples of Asia. The world has become a smaller place today and Asia's economic, cultural and political influence has expanded, yet the need for meaningful dialogue and information about this diverse region has never been greater. Since 1948, Tuttle has been a leader in publishing books on the cultures, arts, cuisines, languages and literatures of Asia. Our authors and photographers have won numerous awards and Tuttle has published thousands of books on subjects ranging from martial arts to paper crafts. We welcome you to explore the wealth of information available on Asia at www.tuttlepublishing.com.

Published by Tuttle Publishing, an imprint of Periplus Editions (HK) Ltd.

www.tuttlepublishing.com

ISBN 978-0-8048-4725-4
(Previously published under Isbn 978-0-8048-4014-9)

Distributed by

North America, Latin America & Europe	Japan	Asia Pacific
Tuttle Publishing	Tuttle Publishing	Berkeley Books Pte. Ltd.
364 Innovation Drive	Yaekari Building, 3rd Floor	61 Tai Seng Avenue #02-12
North Clarendon,	5-4-12 Osaki	Singapore 534167
VT 05759-9436 U.S.A.	Shinagawa-ku	Tel: (65) 6280-1330
Tel: 1 (802) 773-8930	Tokyo 141 0032	Fax: (65) 6280-6290
Fax: 1 (802) 773-6993	Tel: (81) 3 5437-0171	inquiries@periplus.com.sg
info@tuttlepublishing.com	Fax: (81) 3 5437-0755	www.periplus.com
www.tuttlepublishing.com	sales@tuttle.co.jp	
	www.tuttle.co.jp	

20 19 18 17   10 9 8 7 6 5 4 3 2 1

Printed in China   1703CM

A Note to the Learner

When it comes to learning Chinese, practice is essential, of course. This workbook offers you many options for practicing and polishing your language skills, and was designed to be used in conjunction with the book *Basic Mandarin Chinese—Speaking & Listening*. However, it may be used to hone speaking skills no matter which book or course you're using to learn Chinese.

There are no Chinese characters to be found here because you don't need characters to learn to speak Chinese. In fact, learning the characters for everything you learn to say is an inefficient way to learn Chinese, one that significantly slows down your progress.

To help you learn to speak and understand Chinese as efficiently as possible, this workbook gives you the Chinese language portions not via characters, but instead through **audio** featuring native speakers (on the accompanying disc). And in the pages of this book, the Chinese is represented in Hanyu Pinyin, the official Chinese romanization system.

- If you wish to learn Chinese reading and writing, which is certainly to be recommended for most learners, you should—together with or after the spoken course—use the companion course **Basic Mandarin Chinese—Reading & Writing**. It corresponds with *Basic Mandarin Chinese—Speaking & Listening* and systematically introduces the highest-frequency characters (simplified and traditional) and words in context in sentences and reading passages as well as in realia such as street signs, notes, and name cards.

- For instructors and those learners with prior knowledge of Chinese characters, a *Basic Mandarin Chinese—Speaking & Listening* **Character Transcription** is also available. It contains transcriptions into simplified and traditional characters of *Basic Mandarin Chinese—Speaking & Listening*. Please note that the character transcription is not intended, and should not be used, as the primary vehicle for beginning students to learn reading and writing.

- The *Basic Mandarin Chinese* **Instructor's Guide** contains detailed suggestions for using these materials as well as communicative exercises for use by instructors in class or by tutors during practice sessions.

附注

《基础中文：听与说》练习册为专门练习口语的教材，因此全书内只列有汉语拼音和英文注释，不使用汉字。学习者宜与配套的光盘以及《基础中文：听与说》一起使用。本练习册亦可作为任何初级中文课程之补充教材，以提高学习者的口语能力。此套中文教材另有《基础中文：读与写》及《基础中文：读与写》练习册，专供读写课使用。《基础中文：听与说》另配有汉字版，将《基础中文：听与说》中所有对话和补充生词的拼音版转为汉字，并分简繁体，供教师和已有汉字基础的学习者参考、使用。此套教材亦包括一张光盘的《基础中文：教师手册》，指导教师如何使用此教材，且提供大量课堂练习，极为实用。

附注

《基礎中文：聽與說》練習冊為專門練習口語的教材，因此全書內只列有漢語拼音和英文注釋，不使用漢字。學習者宜與配套的光盤以及《基礎中文：聽與說》一起使用。本練習冊亦可作為任何初級中文課程之補充教材，以提高學習者的口語能力。此套中文教材另有《基礎中文：讀與寫》及《基礎中文：讀與寫》練習冊，專供讀寫課使用。《基礎中文：聽與說》另配有漢字版，將《基礎中文：聽與說》中所有對話和補充生詞的拼音版轉為漢字，並分簡繁體，供教師和已有漢字基礎的學習者參考、使用。此套教材亦包括一張光盤的《基礎中文：教師手冊》，指導教師如何使用此教材，且提供大量課堂練習，極為實用。

Do you prefer single-sided pages for ease in turning in completed exercises for review & correction?

See the Disc:

Sections 5, 6, 7, and **8** may be printed out in single-sided format.

Substitution Drills

In the substitution drills, a model sentence is first said for you to repeat. Next, various vocabulary and grammar prompts are given that you're to substitute into the model sentence, creating a related but new sentence.

In the audio portion, after each prompt a pause is provided for the learner to say the new sentence with that substitution. A native speaker then provides a confirmation of the correct sentence, followed by a pause during which you should repeat the correct sentence. An English translation of each sentence is included in the workbook.

- It's most effective to do each drill at least twice: the first time with the workbook open and the second time with the workbook closed.

Transformation and Response Drills

As the name implies, these drills involve transforming one phrase or sentence into another, or responding to a question or other cue. There are also a smaller number of politeness drills, translation drills, and drills involving the conversion of Bejing-style speech to non-Beijing-style speech and vice versa.

In the audio portion, instructions for each drill are given in English before the drill. As with the substitution drills, each of the transformation and response drills is followed by a pause for the learner's response, which is then in turn followed by confirmation of the correct response by a native speaker. A pause then allows you time to repeat the correct sentence. An English translation of each sentence or phrase is included in the workbook.

- Again, it is best to do each drill at least twice—once with the workbook open and once with the workbook closed.

- Though the transformation and response drills are in principle meant to be done by students out of class, some instructors may choose to do some of the drills in class, or some of the drills could be adapted for in-class exercises.

Role Play Exercises

The role play exercises involve conversations between two or more speakers that make use of the new vocabulary, grammar, functions, and situations introduced in the lesson.

There are three to eight role plays for each of the four parts of each unit. In many cases, the role plays are based roughly on the textbook's Basic Conversation but with some of the details changed. Most of the role plays involve two roles (indicated by A and B), with a few involving three roles (A, B, C).

Here in the workbook, the role plays are rendered in English, but they're to be performed in Chinese. The role plays are designed to be done as one of the last activities of each lesson.

- While performing the role plays, you may glance at the English but should try to look up as much as possible when saying the Chinese.

- The role plays should be performed at a fairly rapid clip, so you may wish to practice them in advance (making a few notes is fine, but you should not write out complete translations). The goal isn't laboriously translating word-for-word from English to Chinese but, rather, producing natural Chinese equivalents based on the English cues. The emphasis should be on the *performance* of the role plays. If you find that you're hesitant and choppy in performing a role play, this most likely means you haven't yet attained sufficient mastery of the material.

- If you're learning Chinese in a class, after individual students have performed a role play, the instructor will probably lead the whole class in repeating the lines of the role play one more time together.

- If you're learning Chinese on your own, then the role plays will be especially helpful in giving you practice in using the vocabulary and grammar of the lesson in new combinations. By playing all the roles in a role play exercise, you as an independent learner stand to gain extra benefits for your language skills, enhancing your fluency and becoming flexible in swiftly switching perspectives. Of course, if you're learning with a friend or have access to a native-speaking tutor, then each of you could take one role.

Listening Comprehension Exercises

The listening comprehension exercises involve conversations or monologues which are available on the accompanying disc only, since it is *listening* that we want to practice, not reading.[1] There are two listening passages for each lesson, each approximately the same length as the basic conversations, that is, about 6 to 12 lines total. To provide additional practice in listening comprehension, the passages reuse, in new contexts, the new vocabulary (including the Supplementary Vocabulary) and grammar of the current and previous lessons.

Each listening passage is followed by two to four multiple choice questions on the content of the passage. Based on the recorded passages, you should circle the best response—(A), (B), or (C)—to each of the questions that follows.

- While you work on the listening comprehension exercises, feel free to listen to each passage as many times as needed.

- In a classroom setting, the listening comprehension exercises are best done as homework which students hand in the next day for the instructor to correct, grade, and return. After they have been corrected and returned to students, they can be inserted by the student into a binder for future reference.

- Independent learners will also find the listening comprehension exercises helpful for practice in comprehending new combinations of words and grammar patterns; if they have questions, they can ask a tutor or Chinese friend. It may also be useful to obtain the *Instructor's Guide*, since along with the scripts for the listening comprehension exercises it also includes the correct answers.

Dictation Exercises

The dictation exercises provide practice in listening to and transcribing in Pinyin romanization the sounds of Mandarin, as well as listening comprehension practice involving the classroom expressions, numbers, ages, money amounts, clock times, amounts of time, and dates (days of the week, days of the month, months, and years).

Dictation exercises are included only for some of the lessons in the textbook. The lesson in the textbook that a given dictation exercise is designed to accompany is indicated.

The dictation exercises provide all learners, independent or class-based alike, with additional practice to reinforce the content of the lesson. If you're learning Chinese in a classroom setting, your instructor may suggest that you do the dictation exercises as homework to reinforce what's been covered in class.

- Like the listening comprehension exercises, the dictation exercises are based on audio recordings by native speakers that are available only on the accompanying disc.[2] Instructions are given in English at the beginning of each exercise.

- You may listen to each dictation exercise as many times as you wish.

---

1. Complete scripts of the listening comprehension exercises in Chinese characters are available in the *Instructor's Guide*, which also includes other exercises for in-class use.
2. Scripts of the dictation exercises are also included in the *Instructor's Guide*.

- Also like the listening comprehension exercises, the dictation exercises may be removed from the workbook for correction by the instructor and then may be kept in a binder for reference.

Translation Exercises

The purpose of the translation exercises is to provide you with additional practice in using the grammar patterns and important vocabulary of the unit and to serve as a check of mastery over the material. Completing the translation exercises will be helpful to students in reviewing for the unit tests.

It is recommended that the classroom instructor correct and return the translation exercises to students before the test on the corresponding unit, so that any remaining problems can be identified and addressed in a timely manner. Students should carefully study the instructor's corrections, making sure they understand why any errors occurred, and file the corrected exercises for later reference.

The translation exercises come in two different sets. The first set of translation exercises consists of five sentences *for each of the four Parts* or lessons of each Unit in the textbook, while the second set of translation exercises consists of ten sentences *for each complete Unit* of the textbook. Instructors can decide whether the students in their classes should complete both sets or only one of the two sets. Independent learners would profit from doing both sets of translation exercises and can read out their translations to a tutor or native-speaking friend for correction and comments.

- The sentences should be translated into Pinyin romanization with correct tone marks in the blank space that has been left under each sentence.

- The English in the translation exercises is in some places purposely somewhat stilted, so as to guide the student toward the correct Chinese translation.

- In certain cases, additional instructions have been added in parentheses within or after the English sentence, for example, to be polite or to use or not use certain words or patterns.

- If you've forgotten the Chinese equivalent for an English word or grammar pattern, you can consult the English-Chinese Glossary, Chinese-English Glossary, or Index of Grammatical and Cultural Topics in the back of the *Basic Mandarin Chinese—Speaking & Listening* textbook.

Abbreviations

Word Classes*

A	Adverb
AT	Attributive
AV	Auxiliary Verb
BF	Bound Form
CJ	Conjunction
CV	Coverb
EV	Equative Verb
EX	Expression
I	Interjection
IE	Idiomatic Expression
L	Localizer
M	Measure
MA	Moveable Adverb
N	Noun
NU	Number
P	Particle
PH	Phrase
PR	Pronoun
PT	Pattern
PV	Postverb
PW	Place Word
QW	Question Word
RC	Resultative Compound
RE	Resultative Ending
SN	Surname
SP	Specifier
SV	Stative Verb
TW	Time Word
V	Verb
VO	Verb-Object Compound

Other Abbreviations and Symbols

(B)	Beijing
(T)	Taipei
lit.	literally
SV	Supplementary Vocabulary
AV	Additional Vocabulary
*	(indicates that what follows is incorrect)
/	(separates alternate forms)

* For explanations of the word classes, see the section "Word Classes of Spoken Chinese" in *Basic Mandarin Chinese—Speaking & Listening*.

1. New Vocabulary and Grammar Summaries

Unit 1, Part 1: New Vocabulary and Grammar

Vocabulary

a	(softens sentence) [P]
bàn	take care of, do [V]
dào	to [CV]
huí	go back to [V]
Kē	Ke [SN]
năr	where [QW]
ne	and how about, and what about [P]
nĭ hăo	hi, how are you? [IE]
nĭ	you [PN]
qù	go [V]
shítáng	cafeteria [PW]
shì(r)	matter [N]
sùshè	dormitory [PW]
túshūguăn	library [PW]
Wáng	Wang [SN]
wŏ	I [PN]
yĕ	also, too [A]
yìdiăn(r)	a little [N]

Grammar

A as final particle to soften questions, greetings, and exclamations: **Nĭ dào năr qù a?** "And where might you be going?"

DÀO...QÙ "go to…": **Wáng Jīngshēng dào năr qù?** "Where is Jingsheng Wang going?"

Name + Greeting: **Wáng Jīngshēng, nĭ hăo!** "Jingsheng Wang, how are you?"

Names: **Wáng Jīngshēng** "Jingsheng Wang"

NE as final particle to abbreviate questions: **Wŏ qù shítáng. Nĭ ne?** "I'm going to the dining hall. And what about you?"

QÙ + Place word to indicate "go to a certain place": **Wŏ qù túshūguăn.** "I'm going to the library."

QÙ + Verb to indicate purpose: **Wŏ qù túshūguăn bàn yìdiănr shì.** "I'm going to the library to take care of something."

Question Word Questions: **Nĭ dào năr qù?** "Where are you going?"

Unit 1, Part 2: New Vocabulary and Grammar

Vocabulary

àiren	spouse [N]
bàba	dad [N]
dōu	all, both [A]
hái	still [A]
háizi	child [N]
hǎo	be good [SV]
hǎo jiǔ bú jiànle	long time no see [IE]
hěn	very [A]
le	(indicates changed status or situation) [P]
lèi	be tired [SV]
ma	(indicates questions) [P]
māma	mom [N]
máng	be busy [SV]
tā	he, she [PN]
tāmen	they [PN]
xiān	first [A]
xièxie	thank you [IE]
xíng	be O.K. [V]
yǒu	have [V]
zàijiàn	goodbye [IE]
zěmmeyàng	how, in what way [QW]
Zhào	Zhao [SN]
zǒu	depart [V]

Grammar

MA to transform statements into questions: **Tāmen yě qù shítáng ma?** "Are they going to the dining hall, too?"

Stative Verb Sentences: **Wǒ hěn lèi.** "I'm tired."

Unmarked coordination: **nǐ àiren, háizi** "your spouse and children"

Unit 1, Part 3: New Vocabulary and Grammar

Vocabulary

ǎi	be short [SV]
bù	not [A]
-de	(in **tǐng…-de** "quite, very") [P]
èi	hey, hi [I]
Gāo	Gao [SN]
gāo	be tall [SV]
gōngzuò	work [N]
Hé	He [SN]
jǐnzhāng	be intense [SV]
kéyi	be O.K. [SV]
kùn	be sleepy [SV]
lǎo	be old [SV]
nán	be difficult [SV]
róngyi	be easy [SV]
shì	be [EQ]
tài	too, excessively [A]
tǐng	quite, very [A]
xiǎo	be small [SV]
xuéxí	study, studies [N]
yàngzi	way [N]
Zhōngwén	Chinese language [N]
zuìjìn	recently [TW]

Grammar

Affirmative-Negative Questions: **Zhōngwén nán bu nán?** "Is Chinese hard?"

BÙ to negate verbs: **bù máng** "not be busy," **bù huí sùshè** "not go back to the dormitory"

LǍO and **XIǍO** before monosyllabic surnames: **Lǎo Gāo** "Old Gao," **Xiǎo Wáng** "Little Wang"

Stative Verbs before nouns as adjectives: **lǎo yàngzi** "old way," **hǎo háizi** "good child," **xiǎo shìr** "small matter"

TǏNG…-DE: **tǐng jǐnzhāngde** "quite intense," **tǐng róngyide** "quite easy"

Tone change of **BÙ** to **BÚ** before Tone Four syllables: **bù + qù → bú qù**

Topic-comment construction: **Nǐ gōngzuò máng bu máng?** "Is your work busy or not busy?"

Vocative Expressions: **Xiǎo Liú!** "Little Liu!," **Bàba!** "Dad!"

· ·

Unit 1, Part 4: New Vocabulary and Grammar

Vocabulary

bú kèqi	you're welcome [IE]
děi	must [AV]
huānyíng	welcome [IE]
jìn	enter [V]
lǎoshī	teacher [N]
Lǐ	Li [SN]
Lín	Lin [SN]
màn zǒu	take care [IE]
méi yìsi	not be interesting [PH]
nǐmen	you (plural) [PN]
nín	you (polite) [PN]
qǐng	please [IE]
qǐng jìn	please come in [IE]
qǐng zuò	please sit down [IE]
tàitai	Mrs. [N]
wǒmen	we [PN]
xiānsheng	Mr. [N]
xiáojie	Miss [N]
Xiè	Xie [SN]
xièxie	thank [V]
yǒu yìsi	be interesting [PH]
zuò	sit [V]

Grammar

Imperatives: **Qǐng nín dào túshūguǎn qù.** "Please go to the library."

LE to indicate a changed situation: **Nǐ māma hǎole ma?** "Has your mom gotten well?," **Wǒ bú qùle.** "I'm no longer going."

Pronouns: **wǒ, nǐ, nín, tā, wǒmen, nǐmen, tāmen**

Titles: **Wáng Xiānsheng** "Mr. Wang," **Lǐ Tàitai** "Mrs. Li," **Wáng Xiáojie** "Miss/Ms. Wang," **Lín Lǎoshī** "Teacher Lin"

Unit 2, Part 1: New Vocabulary and Grammar

Vocabulary

Bái	Bai (lit. "white") [SN]
Chén	Chen [SN]
Huáyì	person of Chinese descent [N]
Huáyì Měiguo rén	Chinese-American [PH]
Jiā'nádà	Canada [PW]
jiào	be called or named [EQ]
kěshi	but [MA]
Mǎ	Ma (lit. "horse") [SN]
Mǎláixīyà	Malaysia [PW]
Měiguo	America [PW]
míngzi	name [N]
nèi-	that [SP]
něi-	which [QW]
něiguó	which country [QW]
qǐng wèn	"excuse me," "may I ask" [IE]
rén	person [N]
Rìběn	Japan [PW]
shémme	what [QW]
Táiwān	Taiwan [PW]
tóngxué	classmate [N]
wèi	(polite measure for people) [M]
wèn	ask [V]
Xībānyá	Spain [PW]
Xīnjiāpō	Singapore [PW]
zhèi-	this [SP]
Zhōngguo	China [PW]

Grammar

JIÀO in equative verb sentences: **Wǒ jiào Bái Jiéruì.** "My name is Bai Jierui." **Nǐ jiào shémme míngzi?** "What's your name?"

Nationalities: **Měiguo rén** "American," **Zhōngguo rén** "Chinese," etc.

SHÌ in equative verb sentences: **Wǒ shi Měiguo rén.** "I am (an) American."

ZHÈI- and **NÈI-** as specifiers with the polite measure **WÈI**: **zhèiwèi lǎoshī** "this teacher," **nèiwèi tóngxué** "that classmate"

Unit 2, Part 2: New Vocabulary and Grammar

Vocabulary

bié	don't [AV]
búyào	don't [AV]
chēnghu	address [V]
-de	(indicates possession) [P]
gāoxìng	be happy [SV]
gěi	for [CV]
hǎo	"all right," "O.K." [IE]
huānyíng	welcome [V]
jiào	call (someone a name) [V]
jièshao	introduce [V]
lái	come [V]
nà	in that case [CJ]
nà	that [PN]
ò	"oh" [I]
rènshi	be acquainted with, know [V]
shéi	who, whom [QW]
tóngwū(r)	roommate [N]
xīn	be new [SV]
yīnggāi	should [AV]
zěmme	how [QW]
zhè	this [PN]
zhèmme	like this, in this way, so [A]

Grammar

BIÉ or **BÚYÀO** to indicate negative imperative: **Qǐng nǐ bié qù!** "Please don't go!" **Búyào jiào wǒ Lǎo Wáng!** "Don't call me old Wang!"

DÀO...LÁI: **Qǐng nǐ dào túshūguǎn lái.** "Please come to the library."

-DE to indicate possession: **wǒde gōngzuò** "my work," **nǐde xīn tóngxué** "your new classmate"

...HǍOLE: **Nǐ hái shi jiào wǒ Xiǎo Chén hǎole.** "It would be better if you called me Little Chen."

YÍXIÀ(R) after verbs to make them less abrupt: **jièshao yixiar** "introduce," **lái yixia** "come," **wèn yixia** "ask"

ZHÈ "this" and **NÀ** "that" as pronoun subjects: **Zhè shi Wáng Àihuá, zhè shi Chén Lì** "This is Wang Aihua, this is Chen Li," **Nà shi shéi?** "Who is that?"

Unit 2, Part 3: New Vocabulary and Grammar

Vocabulary

ba	(indicates supposition) [P]
dàshǐguǎn	embassy [PW]
dàxué	university, college [PW]
dānwèi	work unit, organization [PW]
ge	(general measure) [M]
gōngsī	company, firm [PW]
gōngzuò	work [V]
guìxìng	"what's your honorable surname?" [IE]
jiā	(for companies, factories) [M]
nǚshì	madam, lady [N]
tàitai	wife [N]
tóngshì	colleague [N]
wàijiāobù	foreign ministry [PW]
Wú	Wu [SN]
xiānsheng	husband [N]
Xiānggǎng	Hong Kong [PW]
xiàozhǎng	head of a school [N]
xìng	be surnamed [EQ]
xuéxí	learn, study [V]
yī	one, a [NU]
zài	be located at, at [CV]

Grammar

BA to indicate supposition: **Tā shi Yīngguo rén ba** "I suppose she's English." **Nǐ lèile ba?** "You must be tired?"

XÌNG in equative verb sentences: **Wǒ xìng Zhāng.** "My last name is Zhang." **Nǐ xìng shémme?** "What's your last name?"

· ·

Unit 2, Part 4: New Vocabulary and Grammar

Vocabulary

à	"oh" [I]
cuò	be wrong [SV]
-cuò	wrong [RE]
dài	take along, bring [V]
-de	(indicates that what precedes describes what follows) [P]
gǎo	get, do [V]
gǎocuò	get or do something wrong [RC]
gēn	and [CJ]
Hóu	Hou [SN]
jīnglǐ	manager [N]
-le	(indicates completed action) [P]
Luó	Luo [SN]
màoyì	trade [N]
màoyì gōngsī	trading company [PH]
méi	(indicates past negative of action verbs) [AV]
méi guānxi	"never mind" [IE]
míngpiàn	name card, business card [N]
Shī	Shi [SN]
tàitai	married woman, lady [N]
xiānsheng	gentleman [N]
xiáojie	young lady [N]
Yīngguo	England [PW]
Zhōng-Měi	Sino-American [AT]
zǒngjīnglǐ	general manager [N]

Grammar

BÙ DŌU vs. **DŌU BÙ**: **Wǒmen bù dōu shi Měiguo rén.** "We are not all Americans." **Wǒmen dōu bú shi Měiguo rén.** "None of us is American."

-DE to indicate that what precedes describes what follows: **Zhōng-Měi Màoyì Gōngsīde Shī Xiáojie** "Ms. Shi from Sino-American Trading Company"

-LE to indicate completed action: **Wǒ gǎocuòle.** "I got it wrong."

MÉI to indicate past negative of action verbs: **Tāmen méi lái.** "They didn't come."

MÉI DŌU vs. **DŌU MÉI**: **Tāmen méi dōu qù.** "They didn't all go." **Tāmen dōu méi qù.** "None of them went."

Unit 3, Part 1: New Vocabulary and Grammar

Vocabulary

bā	eight [NU]
bān	class [N]
bàn(r)	half [NU]
Déguo	Germany [PW]
èr	two [NU]
Fǎguo	France [PW]
jǐ-	how many [QW]
jiǔ	nine [NU]
liǎng-	two [NU]
liù	six [NU]
nánde	man, male [N]
nánlǎoshī	male teacher [N]
nánshēng	male student [N]
nǚde	woman, female [N]
nǚlǎoshī	female teacher [N]
nǚshēng	female student [N]
qī	seven [NU]
sān	three [NU]
shí	ten [NU]
sì	four [NU]
wǔ	five [NU]
yígòng	in all [A]
yǒu	there is, there are [V]

Grammar

Numbers from one to ten

Place Word + **YǑU** + Noun Phrase to indicate existence: **Bānshang yǒu shíge tóngxué.** "In the class there are ten classmates."

$\cdots\cdots\cdots\cdots\cdots\cdots\cdots\cdots\cdots\cdots\cdots\cdots\cdots$

Unit 3, Part 2: New Vocabulary and Grammar

Vocabulary

ài	love; like [V]
cāi	guess [V]
dà	be big; old (of people) [SV]
dìdi	younger brother [N]
duì	be correct [SV]
duō	how [QW]
fùqin	father [N]
gēge	older brother [N]
jiějie	older sister [N]
jīnnián	this year [TW]
jiù	then [A]
kàn	look, see [V]
kě'ài	be loveable, cute [SV]
méiyou	not have; there is/are not [V]
mèimei	younger sister [N]
mǔqīn	mother [N]
niánji	age [N]
shàng-	last [SP]
suì	year of age [M]
xià-	next [SP]
xiǎng	think [V]
yuè	month [N]

Grammar

Age: **Nǐ duō dà niánji le?** "How old are you?"; **Nǐ jǐsuì le?** "How old are you?" (of children); **Wǒ jīnnián shíbāsuì le.** "I'm eighteen years old."

LE to indicate anticipated change in a situation: **Tā xiàge yuè jiù jiǔsuì le** "Next month she will be nine years old."

MÉIYOU "not have; there is not/there are not" as the negative of **YǑU**: **Wǒ méiyou gēge.** "I don't have (any) older brothers."

Numbers from 11 to 99 with **SHÍ**

Reduplicated monosyllabic verbs + **KÀN**: **xiángxiang kàn** "try and think"

Tag Questions: **Zhè shi nǐ mèimei, duì bu duì?** "This is your younger sister, right?"; **Zhè shi nǐ dìdi, shì bu shi?** "This is your younger brother, isn't it?"

Unit 3, Part 3: New Vocabulary and Grammar

Vocabulary

a	(indicates suggestions) [P]
-bǎi	hundred [NU]
bēibāo	knapsack, backpack [N]
bēizi	cup [N]
dàizi	bag [N]
duōshǎo	how much, how many [QW]
fēn	penny [M]
gōngshìbāo	briefcase, attache case [N]
guì	be expensive [SV]
jiā	add; plus [V]
jiǎn	subtract; minus [V]
kuài	dollar (monetary unit) [M]
líng	zero [NU]
mǎi	buy [V]
mài	sell [V]
máo	ten cents, dime [M]
piányi	be cheap [SV]
-qiān	thousand [NU]
qián	money [N]
yào	want, need, cost, take [V]
yī	one [NU]
yò	"gosh," "wow" [I]
zhǐ	only [A]

Grammar

BA to indicate suggestions: **Nín kàn ba.** "Why don't you take a look?"

LE after **TÀI** in affirmative sentences: **tài guìle** "too expensive"

Monetary system: **liùkuài wǔmáo jiǔfēn qián** "six dollars and fifty-nine cents"

Numbers from 100 to 999 with **-BǍI** "hundred"

Numbers from 1,000 to 9,999 with **-QIĀN** "thousand"

Reduplication of verbs: **kàn → kànkan** "take a look"

YÀO to indicate price: **Nèige bēizi yào sānkuài wǔ.** "That cup costs three fifty."

ZHÈIGE "this/this one" and **NÈIGE** "that/that one"

Unit 3, Part 4: New Vocabulary and Grammar

Vocabulary

chà	lack [V]
chàbuduō	almost, about [MA]
cháng	be long [SV]
chē	vehicle (car, cab, bus, bicycle) [N]
dào	arrive, reach [V]
diǎn	o'clock, hour [M]
fēn	minute [M]
huǒ	fire [N]
huǒchē	train [N]
-jí	reach a goal in time [RE]
kāi	depart (of a train, bus, ship) [V]
kè	quarter of an hour [M]
kǒngpà	"I'm afraid that"; probably [MA]
láibují	not have enough time [RC]
nèmme	then, in that case, well [CJ]
shíjiān	time [N]
tàng	(for runs by trains, buses) [M]
Tiānjīn	Tianjin [PW]
xiànzài	now [TW]
yǐjīng	already [A]
zài	again [A]
zhōng	clock, o'clock; bell [N]
zhōngtóu	hour [N]
zuò	travel by, take [V]

Grammar

Clock times: **liǎngdiǎn sānshibāfēn zhōng** "2:38"

-DE following long phrases to indicate modification: **dào Tiānjīnde huǒchē** "the trains that go to Tianjin"

-DE to create nominal phrases: **shídiǎn bànde** "the 10:30 one," **wǒ mǎide** "the ones I bought"

Number of hours: **sān'ge zhōngtóu** "three hours"

Time when before the verb: **Wǒ bādiǎn zhōng qù.** "I go at eight o'clock."

Unit 4, Part 1: New Vocabulary and Grammar

Vocabulary

guān	close [V]
guānmén	close a door, close [VO]
kāi	open [V]
kāimén	open a door, open [VO]
lǐbài	week [N]
měi-	each, every [SP]
mén(r)	door, gate [N]
náli	"not at all" [IE]
píngcháng	usually, ordinarily [MA]
qǐchuáng	get up from bed, rise [VO]
shàngwǔ	morning, A.M. [TW]
shíyàn	experiment [N]
shíyànshì	laboratory [N]
shuì	sleep [V]
shuìjiào	sleep, go to bed [VO]
tiān	day [M]
wǎnshang	in the evening [TW]
xiàwǔ	afternoon, P.M. [TW]
xīngqī	week [N]
xiūxi	rest, take time off [V]
yǔyán	language [N]
yǔyán shíyànshì	language lab [PH]
zǎoshang	in the morning [TW]

Grammar

Days of the week: **xīngqīyī** OR **lǐbàiyī** "Monday," **xīngqī'èr** OR **lǐbài'èr** "Tuesday," **xīngqīsān** OR **lǐbàisān** "Wednesday," **xīngqīsì** OR **lǐbàisì** "Thursday," **xīngqīwǔ** OR **lǐbàiwǔ** "Friday," **xīngqīliù** OR **lǐbàiliù** "Saturday," **xīngqītiān** OR **xīngqīrì** OR **lǐbàitiān** OR **lǐbàirì** "Sunday," **xīngqījǐ** OR **lǐbàijǐ** "which day of the week?"

TIĀN as measure meaning "day": **yìtiān** "one day," **liǎngtiān** "two days," **jǐtiān** "how many days?," **měitiān** "every day"

Time spent after the verb: **Yǔyán shíyànshì xīngqīliù kāi bàntiān.** "On Saturday the language lab is open for half the day."

Unit 4, Part 2: New Vocabulary and Grammar

Vocabulary

chūshēng	be born [V]
děng	wait, wait for [V]
dìzhǐ	address [N]
dōng	east [L]
duàn	section [M]
gōng	bow (the weapon) [N]
hào	day of the month; number (in addresses, sizes) [M]
hépíng	peace [N]
jīnnián	this year [TW]
jīntiān	today [TW]
jiù	precisely, exactly [A]
lóu	floor (of a building) [N]
Mínguó	the Republic (of China) [TW]
míngnián	next year [TW]
míngtiān	tomorrow [TW]
nián	year [M]
-nòng	alley [BF]
qùnián	last year [TW]
shēngrì	birthday [N]
wénhuà	culture [N]
-xiàng	lane [BF]
Zhāng	Zhang [SN]
zuótiān	yesterday [TW]

Grammar

Addresses: **Zhōngguo Guǎngdōng Guǎngzhōu Zhōngshān Lù wǔhào sānlóu** "3rd floor, Number 5, Zhong Shan Road, Guangzhou, China"

Dates: **èr-líng-líng-wǔ nián shíyīyuè èrhào xīngqīyī** "Monday, November 2, 2005"

Days of the month with **HÀO**: **wǔhào** "the fifth," **jǐhào** "which day of the month?"

Floors of buildings with **LÓU**: **yīlóu** "first floor," **èrlóu** "second floor," **jǐlóu?** "which floor?"

Months of the year with **YUÈ**: **yīyuè** "January," **èryuè** "February," **sānyuè** "March," **sìyuè** "April," **wǔyuè** "May," **liùyuè** "June," **qíyuè** "July," **báyuè** "August," **jiǔyuè** "September," **shíyuè** "October," **shíyīyuè** "November," **shí'èryuè** "December," **jǐyuè** "which month of the year?"

NIÁN as measure for "year": **yìnián** "one year," **jǐnián** "how many years?" **měinián** "every year"

SHI...-DE to express time or place of known past actions: **Wǒ shi yī-jiǔ-bā-wǔ-nián chūshēngde.** "I was born in 1985."

Time when before place: **Wǒ shi yī-jiǔ-bā-wǔ-nián zài Měiguo chūshēngde.** "I was born in 1985 in America."

Years of the calendar with **NIÁN**: **yī-jiǔ-bā-wǔ-nián** "1985"

Unit 4, Part 3: New Vocabulary and Grammar

Vocabulary

báitiān	in the daytime [TW]
cì	time [M]
dàyuē	approximately, about [A]
dì-	(forms ordinal numbers) [SP]
fángjiān	room [N]
-guo	(indicates experience) [P]
hòunián	year after next [TW]
hòutiān	day after tomorrow [TW]
huíguó	return to one's home country [VO]
huíjiā	return to one's home [VO]
jiā	family, home [PW]
jiǔ	be long (of time) [SV]
m	(hesitation sound; pause filler) [I]
qiánnián	year before last [TW]
qiántiān	day before yesterday [TW]
ránhòu	afterward, then [MA]
shuō	say, speak [V]
yào	be going to, will [AV]
yèli	at night [TW]
zhōngwǔ	noon [TW]
zhù	live (in), stay (in) [V]

Grammar

Dì- to create ordinal numbers: **dìyī** "first," **dì'èrge** "the second one," **dìsāncì** "the third time"

-GUO to express experience: **Wǒ qùguo.** "I've gone there." OR "I've been there."

· ·

Unit 4, Part 4: New Vocabulary and Grammar

Vocabulary

-bǎiwàn	million [NU]
Běijīng	Beijing [PW]
bǐjiào	comparatively, relatively [A]
chángcháng	often [A]
chídào	arrive late, be late [V]
duō	be many, much, more [SV]
Guǎngzhōu	Guangzhou, Canton [PW]
hǎoxiàng	apparently, it seems to me [MA]
kè	class [N]
Nánjīng	Nanjing [PW]
-qiānwàn	ten million [NU]
rénkǒu	population [N]
Shànghǎi	Shanghai [PW]
shàngkè	have class [VO]
shǎo	be few, less [SV]
shíwàn	hundred thousand [NU]
Sūn	Sun [SN]
Táiběi	Taipei [PW]
táokè	skip class [VO]
-wàn	ten thousand [NU]
Xī'ān	Xian [PW]
-yì	hundred million [NU]

Grammar

DUŌ to express "more than": **yìbǎiduō rén** "more than a hundred people," **yìqiānduōkuài** "more than a thousand dollars"

HǍOXIÀNG: **Tāmen hǎoxiàng hái méi lái.** "It seems they haven't come yet."

Large numbers: **yíwàn** "ten thousand," **shíwàn** "one hundred thousand," **yìbǎiwàn** "one million," **yìqiānwàn** "ten million," **yíyì** "one hundred million," **shíyì** "billion"

Unit 5, Part 1: New Vocabulary and Grammar

Vocabulary

bǎ	(for chairs, umbrellas) [M]
bàngōngshì	office [PW]
bàoqiàn	feel sorry, regret [V]
búguò	however [CJ]
dāngrán	of course [MA]
Huáqiáo	overseas Chinese [N]
kéyi	may, can [AV]
lǎobǎn	boss, owner [N]
líu	leave (someone something) [V]
nàr	there [PW]
shízài	really, truly [A]
tiáozi	note [N]
xiǎng	want to, would like to [AV]
yàoshi	if [MA]
yǐzi	chair [N]
Yīngwén	English (language) [N]
zài	be present; be located at [V]
zěmme bàn	"what should be done?" [IE]
zhāng	(for tables, name cards) [M]
zhǎo	look for [V]
zhèr	here [PW]
zhīdao	know [V]
zhuōzi	table [N]

Grammar

Deletion of second syllable of bisyllabic verbs in affirmative part of affirmative-negative questions: **kéyi bu kéyi → kě bu kéyi** "may I or may I not?"

Embedded questions: **Nǐ zhīdao tā zài nǎr ma?** "Do you know where she is?"

GĚI as coverb: **Wǒ gěi tā líu yíge tiáozi** "I'm going to leave a note for her."

YÀOSHI: **Yàoshi nǐ zhǎo yíge rén.../Nǐ yàoshi zhǎo yíge rén...** "If you're looking for a person..."

ZÀI as main verb: **Tā zài bu zài?** "Is she present?," **Tā zài Niǔyuē.** "She is in New York."

-ZI as a noun suffix: **zhuōzi** "table," **yǐzi** "chair"

Unit 5, Part 2: New Vocabulary and Grammar

Vocabulary

Běidà	Peking University [PW]
cài	food [N]
cháng	often [A]
chǎng	factory [N]
chī	eat [V]
chīfàn	eat food, eat [VO]
dàxuéshēng	college student [N]
fàn	rice (cooked); food [N]
gōngrén	worker, laborer [N]
Hànyǔ	Chinese (language) [N]
kuài	soon, quickly [A]
péixùn	train [V]
pí	leather, skin [N]
píxié	leather shoe [N]
wǎnfàn	dinner, evening meal [N]
wèizi	seat, place [N]
wǔfàn	lunch [N]
xié	shoe [N]
xué	learn, study [V]
xuésheng	student [N]
zǎofàn	breakfast [N]
zhōngfàn	lunch [N]
zhōngxīn	center [N]

Grammar

College and university abbreviations: **Běijīng Dàxué → Běidà** "Peking University"

KUÀI (YÀO)...LE to indicate an imminent action or situation: **Tā kuài yào zǒule.** "She will be leaving soon."

LÁI + Verb to indicate purpose: **Tā lái zhèr xué Zhōngwén.** "She's coming here to study Chinese."

Verb-Object compounds: **chīfàn** "eat rice, eat," **shuìjiào** "sleep"

ZÀI as coverb: **Wǒ zài yìjiā gōngsī gōngzuò.** "I work at a company."

Unit 5, Part 3: New Vocabulary and Grammar

Vocabulary

bān	move (a thing or one's home) [V]
běibiān(r)	north [PW]
cèsuǒ	toilet [PW]
Cháng Chéng	Great Wall [PW]
Cháng Chéng Fàndiàn	Great Wall Hotel [PW]
chéng	city [N]
-dào	arrive at, to [PV]
dìfang	place [N]
dōngbiān(r)	east [PW]
fàndiàn	hotel [PW]
huí	time [M]
kě	indeed, certainly [A]
méi shì(r)	"it's nothing," "never mind" [IE]
nánbiān(r)	south [PW]
něibiān(r)	which side, where [QW]
nèibian(r)	that side, there [PW]
pàng	be fat (of people or animals) [SV]
ràng	let, cause, make [CV]
ràng nǐ jiǔ děngle	"made you wait a long time" [IE]
shān	mountain, hill [N]
shòu	be thin, lean, skinny [SV]
xībiān(r)	west [PW]
xiāng	be fragrant, smell good [SV]
Xiāng Shān	Fragrant Hills [PW]
yāo	one [NU]
-zài	at, in, on [PV]
zhèibian(r)	this side, here [PW]

Grammar

-DÀO as postverb: **Tāmen qùnián bāndao Táiběi le.** "Last year they moved to Taipei."

Points of the compass: **dōngbiān(r)** "east, east side," **nánbiān(r)** "south, south side," **xībiān(r)** "west, west side," **běibiān(r)** "north, north side"

Stative Verb + **(YÌ)DIǍN(R)**: **piányi yìdiǎnr** "a little cheaper," **hǎo yìdiǎn** "a little better"

-ZÀI as postverb: **Wǒ zhùzai Nánjīng.** "I live in Nanjing."

Unit 5, Part 4: New Vocabulary and Grammar

Vocabulary

āiyò	(indicates surprise) [I]
dǐxia	underneath [PW]
diànnǎo	computer [N]
dōngxi	thing [N]
e	(hesitation sound; pause filler) [I]
gǒu(r)	dog [N]
guǎn	concern oneself with [V]
hòu	in back, back [L]
hòubian(r)/hòumian/hòutou	in back, back [PW]
kāiguān	switch [N]
lǐ	in, inside [L]
lǐbian(r)/lǐmiàn/lǐtou	in, inside [PW]
pángbiān(r)	at or on the side, next to [PW]
qián	in front, front [L]
qiánbian(r)/qiánmian/qiántou	in front, front [PW]
shàng	on top, on [L]
shàngbian(r)/shàngmian/shàngtou	on top, on [PW]
shǐyòng	use, employ [V]
shǐyòng shǒucè	operating manual [PH]
shǒucè	handbook, manual [N]
shūfáng	study [PW]
shūjià	bookshelf, bookcase [N]
tā	it (animal or thing) [PN]
tái	(for computers, TV sets) [M]
wài	outside [L]
wàibian(r)/wàimian/wàitou	outside [PW]
wǔ-bā-liù	Pentium® (brand of computer) [N]
xià	on the bottom, under, below [L]
xiàbian(r)/xiàmian/xiàtou	on the bottom, under, below [PW]
yào	want to [AV]
yòu	right [L]
yòubian(r)	right side, right [PW]
zuǒ	left [L]
zuǒbian(r)	left side, left [PW]

Grammar

-LE in sentences with quantified objects to indicate completed action: **Wǒ mǎile yìtái xīn diànnǎo** "I bought a new computer."

Localizers: **fángjiānli** "in the room," **zhuōzishang** "on the table"

Place Words: **lǐmiàn/lǐtou/lǐbian(r)** "inside"; **wàibian(r)/wàimian/wàitou** "outside"; **qiánbian(r)/qiánmian/qiántou** "in front"; **hòubian(r)/hòumian/hòutou** "in back"; **shàngbian(r)/shàngmian/shàngtou** "on top"; **xiàbian(r)/xiàmian/xiàtou** "on the bottom"; **zuǒbian(r)** "left side," **yòubian(r)** "right side," **pángbiān(r)** "on the side, next to"; **dǐxia** "underneath"

Unit 6, Part 1: New Vocabulary and Grammar

Vocabulary

āyí	aunt (mother's sister) [N]
chū'èr	second year in junior high school [TW]
chūsān	third year in junior high school [TW]
chūyī	first year in junior high school [TW]
chūzhōng	junior high school [PW]
dà'èr	sophomore year in college [TW]
dàsān	junior year in college [TW]
dàsì	senior year in college [TW]
dàyī	first year in college [TW]
gāo'èr	junior year in high school [TW]
gāosān	senior year in high school [TW]
gāoyī	sophomore year in high school [TW]
gāozhōng	senior high school [PW]
-gěi	give; for, to [PV]
hǎochī	be good to eat, delicious [SV]
hǎokàn	be good-looking [SV]
lǐwù	gift, present [N]
m	(indicates something tastes delicious) [I]
nánpéngyou	boyfriend, male friend [N]
niánjí	grade, level (in school) [N]
nǚpéngyou	girlfriend, female friend [N]
péngyou	friend [N]
shàng	go to, attend [V]
shūshu	uncle (father's younger brother) [N]
sòng	give (as a present) [V]
táng	candy; sugar [N]
xǐhuan	like [AV/V]
xiǎoxué	elementary school [PW]
yìniánjí	first grade [TW]
zhēn	really [A]
zhōngxué	middle school [PW]

Grammar

School system and grade in school: **xiǎoxué sānniánjí** "third grade in elementary school," **chūyī** "seventh grade," **gāo'èr** "eleventh grade," **dàsān** "junior year in college," **jǐniánjí** "which grade?"

. . . .

Unit 6, Part 2: New Vocabulary and Grammar

Vocabulary

bānjiā	move one's home [VO]
-dà	big [RE]
ei	(indicates liveliness) [P]
érzi	son [N]
jiéhūn	marry, get married [VO]
Jīn	gold [SN]
jīn	gold [BF]
jiù	be old (of things) [SV]
Jiùjīnshān	San Francisco [PW]
kànqilai	in the looking [RC]
líhūn	divorce, get divorced [VO]
náli	where [QW]
nàli	there [PW]
niánqīng	be young [SV]
Niŭyuē	New York [PW]
nǚ'ér	daughter [N]
-qǐlai	in the VERBing [RE]
xiǎohái(r)	small child, kid [N]
yìsi	meaning [N]
zhǎng	grow [V]
zhǎngdà	grow up [RC]
zhèli	here [PW]
zuò	do, make [V]

Grammar

-QILAI to indicate "in the VERBing": **Tā kànqilai hěn lǎo.** "She looks very old."

Unit 6, Part 3: New Vocabulary and Grammar

Vocabulary

dōngběi	northeast [PW]
dōngnán	southeast [PW]
fúwù	serve [V]
hángkōng	aviation [N]
hángkōng gōngsī	airline [PH]
jiāo	teach [V]
jiāoshū	teach [VO]
Měiguo Zài Tái Xiéhuì	American Institute in Taiwan [PW]
méiyou	(indicates past negative of action verbs) [AV]
néng	be able to, can [AV]
shàngbān(r)	work, go to work [VO]
shàngxué	attend school [VO]
suóyi	therefore, so [CJ]
Táiběi Měiguo Xuéxiào	Taipei American School [PW]
wèishemme	why [QW]
xiàbān(r)	get off from work [VO]
xīběi	northwest [PW]
xī'nán	southwest [PW]
Xī'nán Hángkōng Gōngsī	Southwest Airlines® [PW]
xiéhuì	association, society [N]
xuéxiào	school [PW]
yīnwei	because [MA]

Grammar

Intermediate points of the compass: **dōngnán** "southeast," **dōngběi** "northeast," **xī'nán** "southwest," **xīběi** "northwest"

JIĀO and **JIĀOSHŪ**: **Wǒ xǐhuan jiāoshū.** "I like to teach." **Shéi jiāo nǐmen Yīngwén?** "Who is teaching you English?"

MÉIYOU to indicate past negative of action verbs: **Tā méiyou qù.** "She didn't go."

YĪNWEI...SUÓYI...: **Tā yīnwei hěn máng, suóyi bù néng lái.** "Because she's busy, she can't come."

· ·

Unit 6, Part 4: New Vocabulary and Grammar

Vocabulary

Àodàlìyà	Australia [PW]
Àozhōu	Australia [PW]
dàmèi	older younger sister
fùmǔ	parents [N]
gěi	give [V]
gēn	with [CV]
Huáng	Huang (lit. "yellow") [SN]
jīhui	opportunity, chance [N]
jiěmèi	older and younger sisters [N]
lǎo-	(indicates rank among siblings) [BF]
lǎodà	oldest (among siblings) [N]
liáo	chat [V]
liáotiān	chat [VO]
liúxué	study as a foreign student [VO]
páiháng	one's seniority among siblings [N]
wàizǔfù	maternal grandfather [N]
wàizǔmǔ	maternal grandmother [N]
wàng	forget [V]
xiǎomèi	younger younger sister [N]
xiōngdì	older and younger brothers [N]
yímín	immigrate, emigrate [V]
yǐhòu	in the future [TW]
Zhèng	Zheng [SN]
zìwǒ jièshao	introduce oneself [PH]
zǔfù	paternal grandfather [N]
zǔmǔ	paternal grandmother [N]

Grammar

...-LE...LE in sentences with non-quantified objects to indicate completed action: **Wǒ wàngle zìwǒ jièshaole.** "I forgot to introduce myself."

Unit 7, Part 1: New Vocabulary and Grammar

Vocabulary

biǎojiě	older female cousin of different surname [N]
biǎojiěfu	husband of older female cousin of different surname [N]
cóngqián	in the past, formerly [TW]
gǎiháng	change one's line of work [VO]
gōngchǎng	factory [PW]
hái	in addition [A]
hé	and [CJ]
kǒu	(for people; lit. "mouth") [M]
mǎimài	business [N]
nánháir	boy [N]
ne	(pause filler) [P]
nǚháir	girl [N]
shēntǐ	body [N]
xiàn	county [N]
yòu'éryuán	kindergarten [PW]
yuánlái	originally, formerly [MA]
zuò mǎimài	do or engage in business [PH]

Grammar

Choice-type questions with choice implied: **Nánháir nǚháir?** "A boy or a girl?" **Nǐ yào zhèige yào nèige?** "Do you want this one or do you want that one?"

Unit 7, Part 2: New Vocabulary and Grammar

Vocabulary

Běijīng Yǔyán Wénhuà Dàxué	Beijing Language and Culture University [PW]
bú cuò	"not bad," "quite good" [IE]
Déyǔ	German (language) [N]
-de	(verb suffix that indicates manner) [P]
Fǎyǔ	French (language) [N]
Hànzì	Chinese character [N]
huà	word, language [N]
huì	know how to, can [AV]
jǐ-	a few, several [NU]
jìxù	continue [V]
ma	(indicates something obvious) [P]
Pǔtōnghuà	Mandarin (language) [N]
qítā	other [AT]
quán	completely [A]
rènshi	recognize [V]
Rìyǔ	Japanese (language) [N]
shuōhuà	speak words, speak [VO]
Xībānyáyǔ	Spanish (language) [N]
xiě	write [V]
xiězì(r)	write characters, write [VO]
ya	(form of particle **a** used after words ending in **-a** or **-i**) [P]
yǐqián	before, formerly [TW]
Yīngyǔ	English (language) [N]
yǒude	some [AT]
Zhōngguo huà	spoken Chinese [PH]
Zhōngguo zì(r)	Chinese character [PH]

Grammar

Equivalents of "can": **huì** "know how," **néng** "be physically able," **kéyi** "have permission to"

Equivalents of "know": **huì** "know how," **zhīdao** "know a fact," **rènshi** "be acquainted with"

-DE after verbs to indicate manner: **Tā Zhōngguo huà shuōde hěn hǎo.** "She speaks Chinese very well." **Tā xiě Zhōngguo zì xiěde hěn hǎokàn.** "He writes Chinese characters very attractively."

MA to indicate an obvious situation: **Nínde Hànyǔ shuōde tǐng bú cuò ma!** "You speak Chinese quite well, you know!"

Names of languages

Question words used as indefinites: **Wǒ rènshi jǐbǎige Zhōngguo zì.** "I know a few hundred Chinese characters." **Wǒ zhǐ yǒu jǐkuài qián.** "I only have a few dollars."

Terms for "Chinese language"

YǑUDE...YǑUDE...: **Yǒude láile, yǒude méi lái.** "Some came, some didn't come." **Yǒude wǒ mǎile, yǒude méi mǎi.** "I bought some, I didn't buy others."

Unit 7, Part 3: New Vocabulary and Grammar

Vocabulary

duàn(r)	section, segment, period (of time) [M]
hé	with [CV]
hòulái	afterward, later [TW]
jiǎng	speak, say [V]
jiǎnghuà	speak, talk [VO]
kāishǐ	begin [V]; in the beginning [TW]
nánguài...	no wonder... [PT]
nèmme	like that, so [A]
shíhou(r)	time [N]
yíge rén	by oneself, alone [PH]
yìqǐ	together [A]
yǒude shíhou(r)	sometimes [PH]
yòu	again [A]
yuǎn	be far away [SV]
yuèfen(r)	month [N]

Grammar

HÉ...YÌQǏ and **GĒN...YÌQǏ**: **Wǒmen hé tāmen yìqǐ qù ba!** "Let's go together with them!"

NÁNGUÀI...: **Nánguài nǐde Hànyǔ jiǎngde zhèmme hǎo.** "No wonder that you speak Chinese so well."

SHI...-DE to express attendant circumstances of known past actions: **Wǒ shi hé wǒ àiren yìqǐ láide.** "I came together with my spouse."

Unit 7, Part 4: New Vocabulary and Grammar

Vocabulary

bàng	be great, wonderful [SV]
bìyè	graduate [PT]
chà	be lacking, deficient [SV]
cóng	from [CV]
duōshù	the majority [N]
fùyu	be prosperous [SV]
gǔ	be ancient [SV]
jiù	only [A]
juéde	feel [V]
nèiyang(r)	that way, like that [MA]
niàn	study [V]
nǔlì	be diligent, work hard [SV]
shēnqǐng	apply [V]
tīngshuō	hear of, hear it said that [V]
yánjiū	research [V/N]
yánjiūshēng	graduate student [N]
...yǐhòu	after... [PT]
...yǐqián	before..., ...ago [PT]
zhèiyang(r)	this way, like this [MA]
...zhīhòu	after... [PT]
...zhīqián	before..., ...ago [PT]
zhì'ān	public order, public security [N]

Grammar

Backchannel comments: **Ò.** "Oh," **Zhèiyang.** "So this is how it is."

BÌYÈ: Tā shi Běidà bìyède. "She graduated from Peking University."

Phrase + **YǏQIÁN/ZHĪQIÁN** and Phrase + **YǏHÒU/ZHĪHÒU: Tā shi yìnián yǐqián qù Zhōngguode.** "He went to China one year ago." **Tā liǎngge yuè zhīhòu yào jiéhūn.** "She's going to get married in two months."

Unit 8, Part 1: New Vocabulary and Grammar

Vocabulary

běi	north [L]
běifāng	north, the North [PW]
běifāng huà	northern speech [PH]
běifāng rén	Northerner [PH]
Běijīng Fàndiàn	Beijing Hotel [PW]
dǎdī	take a taxi [VO]
dàgài	probably, about [MA]
dōngfāng	east, the East [PW]
Dōngfāng rén	Asian person [PH]
gèng	even more, more [A]
guò	pass, go by [V]
huòzhě	or [CJ]
jìn	be close, near [SV]
kāi	drive, operate a vehicle [V]
kuài	be fast [SV]
láojià	excuse me [IE]
lí	be distant from, from [CV]
nán	south [L]
nánfāng	south, the South [PW]
nánfāng huà	southern speech [PH]
nánfāng rén	Southerner [PH]
Tiān'ānmén	Tiananmen [PW]
wàng	to, toward [CV]
xī	west [L]
xīfāng	west, the West [PW]
Xīfāng rén	Westerner [PH]
yìzhí	straight [A]
zǒu	go, walk [V]
zǒulù	walk [VO]
zuǒyòu	about, approximately [PW]

Grammar

Conditional clauses with **-DE HUÀ**: **Zǒulùde huà, dàgài yào bàn'ge zhōngtóu zuǒyòu.** "If you walk, it will probably take about half an hour."

LÍ to express distance from: **Nǐ jiā lí zhèr yuǎn bu yuǎn?** "Is your home far from here?" **Wǒ jiā lí zhèr hěn jìn.** "My home is close to here."

QÙ...ZĚMME ZŎU: Láojià, qù Wàijiāobù zěmme zǒu? "Excuse me, how do you get to the Foreign Ministry?"

WÀNG to express movement toward a certain direction: **wàng xī zǒu** "walk toward the west," **wàng qián kāi** "drive forward"

ZUǑYÒU: liǎngge yuè zuǒyòu "about two months"

Unit 8, Part 2: New Vocabulary and Grammar

Vocabulary

Běijīng Wàiguoyǔ Dàxué	Beijing Foreign Studies University [PW]
Běiwài	(abbreviation for Beijing Foreign Studies University) [PW]
bīnguǎn	guest house, hotel [PW]
chēzi	car, vehicle [N]
chūzū	rent out [V]
chūzū qìchē	taxi [PH]
Fù	Fu [SN]
hǎode	"all right," "O.K." [IE]
jīchǎng	airport [PW]
liàng	(for land vehicles) [M]
lóu	building (with two or more floors) [N]
ménkǒu(r)	doorway, entrance [PW]
qìchē	car, vehicle [N]
shǒudū	capital [N]
Shǒudū Jīchǎng	Capital Airport [PW]
wàiguo	foreign country [N]
wàiguo huà	foreign language [PH]
wàiguo rén	foreigner [PH]
wàiguoyǔ	foreign language [N]
wéi	"hello" [I]
xìngmíng	first and last name [N]
yǒuyì	friendship [N]
Yǒuyì Bīnguǎn	Friendship Hotel [PW]
zhuānjiā	expert [N]
zhuānjiā lóu	(foreign) experts' building [PH]

Grammar

Pivot sentences: **Wǒ yào yíliàng chē qù Shǒudū Jīchǎng** "I want a car to go to Capital Airport"

Unit 8, Part 3: New Vocabulary and Grammar

Vocabulary

dǎ	hit [V]
dǎ diànhuà	make a telephone call [PH]
diànhuà	telephone [N]
fázi	means, method, way [N]
gǎn	rush, hurry [V]
huì	be likely to, will [AV]
jiāotōng	traffic [N]
jìnkuài	as fast as possible [A]
juédìng	decide [V]
máfan	trouble, disturb [V]
mǎshàng	immediately, right away [A]
nàixīn	be patient/patience [SV/N]
pài	dispatch, send [V]
pàiqu	dispatch, send out [RC]
-qu	(indicates motion away from the speaker) [RE]
shàng	go to, come to, to [CV]
sījī	driver, chauffeur [N]
tōngzhī	notify [V]
xiǎoshí	hour [N]
yào	need to, have to, should [AV]; request [V]
yìhuǐr	a while [N]
yōngjǐ	be crowded [SV]
zěmme	how come, why [QW]
zháojí	worry, get excited [SV/VO]

Grammar

Resultative compounds: **pàiqu** "send out," **láibují** "not be able to make it on time"

Unit 8, Part 4: New Vocabulary and Grammar

Vocabulary

bàntiān	"half the day," a long time [NU+M]
biéde	other, another [AT]
dǔchē	be clogged up with cars [VO]
gōngjīn	kilo [M]
huàn	change to, exchange [V]
jiàn	(for luggage, matters) [M]
kāichē	drive a car [VO]
mǐ	meter [M]
qīng	be light (not heavy) [SV]
sāichē	be clogged up with cars [VO]
shīfu	master; driver [N]
tiáo	(for streets, alleys) [M]
xíngli	luggage, baggage [N]
xūyào	need [V]
yīngdāng	should, ought to [AV]
zāogāo	be a mess [SV]; "darn it," "what a mess" [IE]
zhǎo	give in change [V]
zhǎoqián	give (someone) change [VO]
zhǐhǎo	have no choice but [A]
zhòng	be heavy [SV]
zuìhòu	in the end, finally [TW]

Grammar

CÓNG...DÀO...: **Cóng sāndiǎn bàn dào wǔdiǎn.** "From 3:30 until 5:00."

Height and weight: **Nǐ duō zhòng?** "How heavy are you?" **Wǒ liùshisāngōngjīn.** "I weigh 63 kilos." **Nǐ duō gāo?** "How tall are you?" **Wǒ yīmǐ bā'èr.** "I'm one meter eighty-two."

Specifier + Number + Measure + Noun: **zhèiliǎngjiàn xíngli** "these two pieces of luggage"

ZHǏHǍO: **Wǒmen zhǐhǎo huí sùshè.** "We have no choice but to return to our dorm."

Unit 9, Part 1: New Vocabulary and Grammar

Vocabulary

bái	be white [SV]
báisè	the color white [N]
běndì	this place, here [N]
bú yòng	not need to, don't need to [AV]
bú yòng xiè	"don't mention it" [IE]
dēng	light, lamp [N]
guǎi	turn [V]
hēi	be black [SV]
hēisè	the color black [N]
Hépíng Bīnguǎn	Peace Hotel [PW]
hóng	be red [SV]
hónglǜdēng	traffic light [N]
hóngsè	the color red [N]
huáng	be yellow [SV]
huángsè	the color yellow [N]
jiāotōng jǐngchá	traffic police [PH]
jiāotōngjǐng	traffic police [N]
jǐngchá	police [N]
lán	be blue [SV]
lánsè	the color blue [N]
lùkǒu(r)	intersection [PW]
lǜ	be green [SV]
lǜsè	the color green [N]
qīngchu	be clear, clear about [SV]
xiè	thank [V]
yánsè	color [N]
zhuǎn	turn [V]

Grammar

Chinese equivalents of English "ask": **Nǐ yàoshi bù dǒngde huà, yào wèn lǎoshī a!** "If you don't understand, you should ask the teacher!" **Qǐng tā míngtiān zài lái.** "Ask him to come again tomorrow." **Lǎoshī jiào wǒmen zuò zuòyè.** "The teacher asked us to do our homework."

Color terms

Unit 9, Part 2: New Vocabulary and Grammar

Vocabulary

búbì	don't need to, not be necessary [AV]
chēzhàn	bus stop; bus station [PW]
diànchē	street car, trolley, tram [N]
dòngwù	animal [N]
dòngwùyuán(r)	zoo [PW]
gōnggòng	public [AT]
gōnggòng qìchē	public bus, bus [PH]
lù	(for bus routes) [M]
māo(r)	cat [N]
niǎo(r)	bird [N]
shàngchē	get on a vehicle [VO]
yǎng	raise, keep [V]
Yíhéyuán	Summer Palace [PW]
yú(r)	fish [N]
zhàn	station, stop [N]
zhī	(for most animals) [M]
zhōngdiǎn	final or terminal point [N]
zhōngdiǎn zhàn	last station, last stop [PH]

Grammar

XIĀN...RÁNHÒU... "First...then...": **Xiān chīfàn ránhòu zài qù mǎi dōngxi.** "First eat and then go shopping."

Unit 9, Part 3: New Vocabulary and Grammar

Vocabulary

bèn	be stupid [SV]
búdàn	not only [A]
cōngming	be smart [SV]
érqiě	moreover, and, also [CJ]
gānjìng	be clean [SV]
gāng	just now, just [A]
gānggāng	just now, just [A]
jiào	call (someone) [V]
kāi wánxiào	joke around, play a prank [PH]
lǎn	be lazy [SV]
luàn	be disorderly, messy [SV]
méi	not have [V]
piào	ticket [N]
shàng	get on [V]
shēngqì	get angry [SV/VO]
shòupiàoyuán	ticketseller, conductor [N]
shuō xiàohua(r)	tell a joke [PH]
wánxiào	joke [N]
xīwàng	hope [V]
yònggōng	be hardworking, studious [SV]
zāng	be dirty [SV]
zhěngqí	be in order, neat [SV]

Grammar

BÚDÀN...ÉRQIĚ... "Not only...but also...": **Tā búdàn niánqīng, érqiě cōngming.** "She's not only young, but also smart."

Unit 9, Part 4: New Vocabulary and Grammar

Vocabulary

chēpiào	bus ticket [N]
chūshì	show, produce [V]
-dào	(indicates action of verb is realized) [RE]
dǒng	understand [V]
-dǒng	understand [RE]
gāi	should [AV]
jìde	remember [V]
kàn	read [V]
kàndǒng	read and understand [RC]
ne	(indicates continuous aspect) [P]
shuìzháo	fall asleep [RC]
tīng	hear, listen [V]
tīngdǒng	hear and understand [RC]
tóngzhì	comrade [N]
wèi	"hey" [I]
xiàchē	get off a vehicle [VO]
xiǎoxīn	be careful [SV]
yuèpiào	monthly ticket [N]
zǎo	be early [SV]
-zháo	(indicates action of verb is realized) [RE]
zhǎodào	look for and find, find [RC]
zhǎozháo	look for and find, find [RC]
-zhe	(indicates continuous aspect) [P]
zhǔnbèi	prepare, get ready, plan [V]

Grammar

Potential resultative compounds: **zhǎo** "look for," **zhǎozháo** "look for and find," **zhǎodezháo** "be able to find," **zhǎobuzháo** "be unable to find"

-ZHE as continuous aspect suffix: **zǎozhe ne** "it's (continuing being) early"

Unit 10, Part 1: New Vocabulary and Grammar

Vocabulary

āiyà	"oh," "gosh" [I]
biàn	change [V]
-chéng	become; into [PV]
dǎléi	thunder [VO]
dī	be low [SV]
dù	degree (of temperature) [M]
éi	(introduces questions) [I]
...éryǐ	only [PT]
kěnéng	be possible [AV]
qíngtiān	fine day, sunny day [N]
rè	be hot [SV]
shǎndiàn	lightning strikes [VO]
suóyi shuō	so, therefore [PH]
tiān	sky [N]
tiānqi	weather [N]
tiānqi yùbào	weather forecast [PH]
wēndù	temperature [N]
xiàyǔ	rain [VO]
yídìng	definitely [A]
yīntiān	cloudy or overcast weather [N]
yǔ	rain [N]
yùbào	forecast [N]
yuè lái yuè...	more and more... [PT]
yún	cloud [N]
zǎo	"good morning" [IE]
zhǔn	be accurate [SV]
zuì	most [A]

Grammar

CÓNG...KĀISHǏ: cóng míngtiān kāishǐ "starting from tomorrow"

DÙ to express temperatures: **shíbādù** "eighteen degrees"

...ÉRYǏ "and that's all": **Wǒ zhǐ yǒu yìbǎikuài éryǐ.** "I only have one hundred dollars and that's all."

YUÈ LÁI YUÈ... "more and more": **Tiānqi yuè lái yuè rè.** "The weather has been getting hotter and hotter."

. . . .

Unit 10, Part 2: New Vocabulary and Grammar

Vocabulary

chū tàiyáng	the sun comes/is out [PH]
chūntiān	spring [TW]
dōngtiān	winter [TW]
fēng	wind [N]
fēngshā	wind and sand; blowing sand [N]
gān	be dry [SV]
héshì	be appropriate [SV]
hěn shǎo	seldom [PH]
jìjié	season [N]
lěng	be cold [SV]
qiūtiān	fall, autumn [TW]
rúguǒ	if [MA]
shā	sand, gravel [N]
shūfu	be comfortable [SV]
sǐ	die [V]
tàiyáng	sun [N]
wán(r)	play, have a good time [V]
xiàtiān	summer [TW]
xiàxuě	snow [VO]
xuě	snow [N]
yào	if [MA]
zhèmme shuō	saying it like this; then [PH]
zhèng	just [A]

Grammar

BÙ...YĚ BÙ... "neither...nor...": **Tā shuō Zhōngwén bù nán yě bù róngyi.** "She said that Chinese was neither hard nor easy."

RÚGUǑ...JIÙ... "if...then...": **Rúguǒ xiàyǔde huà, wǒmen jiù bú qù.** "If it should rain, we (then) won't go."

YÒU...YÒU... "both...and...": **Nèige xuésheng yòu cōngming yòu yònggōng.** "That student is both smart and diligent."

Unit 10, Part 3: New Vocabulary and Grammar

Vocabulary

bànfǎ(r)	way of doing something, method [N]
cháoshī	be humid [SV]
chūlái	come out [RC]
-chūlái	come out [RE]
chūmén(r)	go outside [VO]
chūqu	go out [RC]
dànshi	but [CJ]
gēnběn (+ NEGATIVE)	(not) at all [A]
jìnlái	come in [RC]
-jìnlái	come in [RE]
jìnqu	go in [RC]
kànchūlái	know something by looking [RC]
kōngqì	air [N]
m	(indicates agreement) [I]
máomáoyǔ	light rain [N]
nèiyangzi	that way, like that [MA]
pèng	bump, run into [V]
pèngshang	run into, meet with, encounter [RC]
piāo	float [V]
piāojìnlái	float in [RC]
qíshí	actually [MA]
shāchuāng	screen window [N]
-shàng	up, on [RE]
táifēng	typhoon [N]
wù	fog [N]
xià máomáoyǔ	drizzle [PH]
Yángmíng Shān	Yangming Mountain [PW]
yùnqi	luck [N]
zài	(indicates progressive aspect) [AV]
zhèiyangzi	this way, like this [MA]

Grammar

Directional Verbs: **jìnlái** "come in," **jìnqu** "go in," **chūlái** "come out," **chūqu** "go out," **piāojìnlái** "float in," **kànbuchūlái** "be unable to know something by looking"

HǍOXIÀNG...-DE YÀNGZI "seem like...": **Hǎoxiàng wù cóng shāchuāng piāojìnláide yàngzi.** "It seems as though the fog is floating in through the window screen."

Noun suffix **-FǍ** "way of doing something": **bànfǎ** "way of doing something," **kànfǎ** "way of looking at things," **xiǎngfǎ** "way of thinking," **xiěfǎ** "way of writing," etc.

Reduplication of measures and nouns to indicate "every": **tiān** "day" → **tiāntiān** "every day," **nián** "year" → **niánnián** "every year," **rén** "person" → **rénrén** "everybody"

ZÀI as auxiliary verb to indicate progressive aspect: **Tā zài chīfàn.** "He's eating."

Unit 10, Part 4: New Vocabulary and Grammar

Vocabulary

Àomén	Macao [PW] (10-4)
bǐ	compare [CV/V]
chàbuduō	not lack much, be good enough [IE]
...-de shíhou(r)	when... [PT]
dōngàn	east coast [PW]
dōng-nuǎn-xià-liáng	"warm in winter, cool in summer" [EX]
fēngjǐng	scenery [N]
gānzào	be dry [SV]
Jiāzhōu	California [PW]
liángkuai	be comfortably cool [SV]
měi	be beautiful [SV]
Měijí Huárén	Chinese with U.S. nationality [PH]
nánguò	be sad [SV]
nuǎnhuo	be warm [SV]
qìhou	climate [N]
shìyìng	adapt, get used to [V]
wǎn	be late [SV]
xī'àn	west coast [PW]
xíguàn	be accustomed to [V]

Grammar

Bǐ to express unequal comparison: **Tā bǐ wǒ gāo.** "He is taller than me."

...DE SHÍHOU(R) "when": **Tā gàosu wǒde shíhou, yǐjīng tài wǎnle.** "When he told me, it was already too late."

A **MÉIYOU** B **NÈMME/ZHÈMME** C "A is not as C as B": **Wǒ méiyou tā nèmme gāo.** "I'm not as tall as him."

2. Substitution Drills
· ·
Unit 1, Part 1: Substitution Drills

Listen to the audio; after each prompt, say the new sentence using that substitution. Do each drill at least twice: first with the book open, then with the book closed. Each drill starts with a model sentence for you to repeat.

---

1. **Kē Léi'ēn**   , nǐ hǎo!   Ke Leien, how are you?
   Wáng Jīngshēng   Wang Jingsheng, how are you?
   Kē Léi'ēn   Ke Leien, how are you?

---

2. **Nǐ**   dào nǎr qù a?   Where are you going?
   Kē Léi'ēn   Where is Ke Leien going?
   Wáng Jīngshēng   Where is Wang Jingsheng going?
   Nǐ   Where are you going?

---

3. Wǒ qù   **túshūguǎn.**   I'm going to the library.
            shítáng.   I'm going to the dining hall.
            sùshè.   I'm going to the dormitory.
            túshūguǎn.   I'm going to the library.

---

4. Wǒ dào   **túshūguǎn**   qù.   I'm going to the library.
            shítáng   I'm going to the cafeteria.
            sùshè   I'm going to the dormitory.
            túshūguǎn   I'm going to the library.

---

5. Wǒ qù túshūguǎn.   **Nǐ**   ne?   I'm going to the library. How about you?
            Kē Léi'ēn   I'm going to the library. How about Ke Leien?
            Wáng Jīngshēng   I'm going to the library. How about Wang Jingsheng?
            Nǐ   I'm going to the library. How about you?

---

6. Wǒ huí   **sùshè.**   I'm going back to the dormitory.
            túshūguǎn.   I'm going back to the library.
            shítáng.   I'm going back to the cafeteria.
            sùshè.   I'm going back to the dormitory.

---

7. **Wǒ**   qù bàn yìdiǎnr shìr.   I'm going to take care of a little matter.
   Kē Léi'ēn   Ke Leien is going to take care of a little matter.
   Wáng Jīngshēng   Wang Jingsheng is going to take care of a little matter.
   Wǒ   I'm going to take care of a little matter.

---

8. Wǒ qù,   **Wáng Jīngshēng yě qù.**   I'm going and Wang Jingsheng is going, too.
            Kē Léi'ēn yě qù.   I'm going and Ke Leien is going, too.
            nǐ yě qù.   I'm going and you're going, too.
            Wáng Jīngshēng yě qù.   I'm going and Wang Jingsheng is going, too.

• •

Unit 1, Part 2: Substitution Drills

Listen to the audio; after each prompt, say the new sentence using that substitution. Do each drill at least twice: first with the book open, then with the book closed. Each drill starts with a model sentence for you to repeat.

1. **Zhào Guócái**	**, hǎo jiǔ bú jiànle!**	Zhao Guocai, long time no see!
Wáng Jīngshēng		Wang Jingsheng, long time no see!
Kē Léi'ēn		Ke Leien, long time no see!
Bàba		Dad, long time no see!
Māma		Mom, long time no see!
Háizi		Child, long time no see!
Zhào Guócái		Zhao Guocai, long time no see!

2. **Nǐ**	**zěmmeyàng a?**	How are you?
Tā		How is he?
Tāmen		How are they?
Nǐ àiren		How is your spouse?
Wáng Jīngshēng		How is Wang Jingsheng?
Shítáng		How is the cafeteria?
Nǐ		How are you?

3. **Wǒ**	**hái xíng.**	I'm all right.
Nǐ		You're all right.
Tā		He's all right.
Tāmen		They're all right.
Wǒ bàba		My dad is all right.
Wǒ māma		My mom is all right.
Wǒ àiren		My spouse is all right.
Wǒ		I'm all right.

4. **Nǐ àiren**	**hǎo ma?**	Is your spouse well?
Nǐ māma		Is your mom well?
Nǐ		Are you well?
Tā		Is she well?
Tāmen		Are they well?
Zhào Guócái		Is Zhao Guocai well?
Sùshè		Is the dormitory good?
Nǐ àiren		Is your spouse well?

5. **Nǐ àiren, háizi**	**dōu hǎo ma?**	Are your spouse and children all O.K.?
Nǐ bàba, māma		Are your mom and dad both O.K.?
Kē Léi'ēn, Wáng Jīngshēng		Are Ke Leien and Wang Jingsheng both O.K.?
Zhào Guócái, Wáng Jīngshēng		Are Zhao Guocai and Wang Jingsheng both O.K.?
Tāmen		Are they all O.K.?
Háizi		Are the children all O.K.?
Nǐ àiren, háizi		Are your spouse and children all O.K.?

6. **Nǐ**	**bàba qù ma?**	Is your father going?
Tā		Is her father going?
Wǒ		Is my father going?
Nǐ		Is your father going?

7. **Tāmen dōu hěn**	**hǎo.**	They are all very well.
	máng.	They are all very busy.
	lèi.	They are all very tired.
	hǎo.	They are all very well.

8. **Tāmen yě dōu**	**hěn hǎo.**	They also are all very well.
	hěn máng.	They also are all very busy.
	qù.	They also are all going.
	huí sùshè.	They also are all going back to the dormitory.
	hái xíng.	They also are all alright.
	yǒu yìdiǎnr shì.	They also all have something to do.
	qù bàn yìdiǎnr shì.	They also are all going to take care of something.
	hěn hǎo.	They also are all very well.

9. **Wǒ**	**yǒu yìdiǎnr shì.**	I have something to do.
Tā		He has something to do.
Tāmen		They have something to do.
Zhào Guócái		Zhao Guocai has something to do.
Wǒ bàba		My father has something to do.
Wǒ		I have something to do.

Unit 1, Part 3: Substitution Drills

Listen to the audio; after each prompt, say the new sentence using that substitution. Do each drill at least twice: first with the book open, then with the book closed. Each drill starts with a model sentence for you to repeat.

1. Èi, Lǎo	Hé	, nǐ hǎo a!	Hey, Old He, how are you?
	Kē		Hey, Old Ke, how are you?
	Wáng		Hey, Old Wang, how are you?
	Gāo		Hey, Old Gao, how are you?
	Zhào		Hey, Old Zhao, how are you?
	Hé		Hey, Old He, how are you?

2. Xiǎo	Gāo	, zuìjìn zěmmeyàng a?	Little Gao, how have you been recently?
	Hé		Little He, how have you been recently?
	Kē		Little Ke, how have you been recently?
	Wáng		Little Wang, how have you been recently?
	Zhào		Little Zhao, how have you been recently?
	Gāo		Little Gao, how have you been recently?

3. Wǒ bù	máng.	I'm not busy.
	jǐnzhāng.	I'm not nervous.
	lǎo.	I'm not old.
	ǎi.	I'm not short.
	zǒu.	I'm not leaving.
	máng.	I'm not busy.

4. Tā yě bú	kùn.	He is also not sleepy.
	lèi.	He is also not tired.
	zuò.	He is also not sitting.
	jìn.	He is also not entering.
	qù.	He is also not going.
	kùn.	He is also not sleepy.

5. Bú tài	máng.	Not very busy.
	lèi.	Not very tired.
	kùn.	Not very sleepy.
	gāo.	Not very tall.
	lǎo.	Not very old.
	nán.	Not very difficult.
	máng.	Not very busy.

6. Nǐ gōngzuò	máng bu máng?	Is your work busy or not?
	lèi bu lèi?	Is your work tiring or not?
	nán bu nán?	Is your work difficult or not?
	jǐnzhāng bu jǐnzhāng?	Is your work intense or not?
	róngyi bu róngyi?	Is your work easy or not?
	máng bu máng?	Is your work busy or not?

7. Tāmen zuìjìn tǐng	jǐnzhāng	de.	They have been quite nervous recently.
	lèi		They have been quite tired recently.
	kùn		They have been quite sleepy recently.
	máng		They have been quite busy recently.
	hǎo		They have been quite well recently.
	jǐnzhāng		They have been quite nervous recently.

- -
Unit 1, Part 4: Substitution Drills

Listen to the audio; after each prompt, say the new sentence using that substitution. Do each drill at least twice: first with the book open, then with the book closed. Each drill starts with a model sentence for you to repeat.

1. **Lín Tàitai**	, xièxie nín le!	Thank you, Mrs. Lin!
Wáng Xiānsheng		Thank you, Mr. Wang!
Zhào Xiáojie		Thank you, Miss Zhao!
Xiè Tàitai		Thank you, Mrs. Xie!
Hé Xiānsheng		Thank you, Mr. He!
Lín Tàitai		Thank you, Mrs. Lin!

2. **Wáng Xiānsheng, qǐng**	**jìn!**	Mr. Wang, please enter!
	màn zǒu!	Mr. Wang, please take care!
	zuò!	Mr. Wang, please sit down!
	qù shítáng!	Mr. Wang, please go to the cafeteria!
	huí sùshè!	Mr. Wang, please return to the dormitory!
	jìn!	Mr. Wang, please enter!

3. **Xiǎo Zhào, qǐng nǐ**	**dào shítáng qù.**	Little Zhao, please go to the cafeteria.
	dào túshūguǎn qù.	Little Zhao, please go to the library.
	huí sùshè.	Little Zhao, please return to the dormitory.
	qù bàn yìdiǎnr shì.	Little Zhao, please go and take care of something.
	xièxie tāmen.	Little Zhao, please thank them.
	qù.	Little Zhao, please go.
	zǒu.	Little Zhao, please leave.
	dào shítáng qù.	Little Zhao, please go to the cafeteria.

4. **Wǒ**	**zǒu**	**le.**	I'll be going now.
	yǒu		I have it now.
	kùn		I've gotten sleepy.
	lèi		I've gotten tired.
	lǎo		I've gotten old.
	hǎo		I'm O.K. now.
	kéyi		I'm O.K. now.
	zǒu		I'll be going now.

5. **Wǒ**	**bú qù**	**le.**	I'm no longer going.
	bú zuò		I won't sit any longer.
	bú bàn		I don't handle it any more.
	bù zǒu		I'm not leaving anymore.
	bù xíng		I'm in a bad way now.
	bú kùn		I'm no longer tired.
	bù jǐnzhāng		I'm no longer nervous.
	bú qù		I'm no longer going.

6. Nǐ	**lèi**	le ma?	Have you gotten tired?
	kùn		Have you gotten sleepy?
	hǎo		Are you O.K. now?
	bú qù		Are you no longer going?
	bú bàn		Are you no longer doing it?
	lèi		Have you gotten tired?

7. Zhōngwén	**yǒu yìsi**	ma?	Is Chinese interesting?
	méi yìsi		Is Chinese not interesting?
	nán		Is Chinese difficult?
	róngyi		Is Chinese easy?
	yǒu yìsi		Is Chinese interesting?

8. **Tāmen**	gāo ma?	Are they tall?
Wǒ		Am I tall?
Nǐ		Are you tall?
Nín		Are you tall?
Tā		Is he tall?
Wǒmen		Are we tall?
Nǐmen		Are you tall?
Tāmen		Are they tall?

Unit 2, Part 1: Substitution Drills

Listen to the audio; after each prompt, say the new sentence using that substitution. Do each drill at least twice: first with the book open, then with the book closed. Each drill starts with a model sentence for you to repeat.

1. **Nǐ**	shi něiguó rén?	What country are you from?
Nín		What country are you from?
Tā		What country is she from?
Xiǎo Hé		What country is Little He from?
Lǎo Zhào		What country is Old Zhao from?
Bái Xiáojie		What country is Miss Bai from?
Xiè Tàitai		What country is Mrs. Xie from?
Nǐ		What country are you from?
2. **Tā shi**	**Zhōngguo rén.**	She is Chinese.
	Jiā'nádà rén.	She is Canadian.
	hǎo háizi.	She is a good child.
	Zhōngwén lǎoshī.	She is a Chinese teacher.
	wǒ bàba.	He is my father.
	wǒ àiren.	She is my spouse.
	hǎo rén.	She is a good person.
	Zhōngguo rén.	She is Chinese.
3. **Nǐ shì bu shi**	**Zhōngguo rén?**	Are you Chinese?
	zǒngjīnglǐ?	Are you the general manager?
	Jiā'nádà rén?	Are you Canadian?
	Měiguo rén?	Are you American?
	Rìběn rén?	Are you Japanese?
	jīnglǐ?	Are you the manager?
	Zhōngguo rén?	Are you Chinese?
4. **Wǒ bú shi**	**Zhōngguo rén.**	I'm not Chinese.
	Táiwān rén.	I'm not Taiwanese.
	Xībānyá rén.	I'm not Spanish.
	Yīngguo rén.	I'm not English.
	lǎoshī.	I'm not a teacher.
	jīnglǐ.	I'm not the manager.
	zǒngjīnglǐ.	I'm not the general manager.
	Zhōngguo rén.	I'm not Chinese.
5. **Nǐ**	jiào shémme míngzi?	What is your name?
Tā		What is her name?
Nǐ māma		What is your mother's name?
Zhèiwèi tóngxué		What is this student's name?
Nèiwèi lǎoshī		What is that teacher's name?
Nǐ		What is your name?

6.	Tā	jiào	shémme?	What is his name?
		wèn		What did he ask?
		bàn		What is he taking care of?
		yǒu		What does he have?
		jiào		What is his name?

7.	Nǐmen dōu shi	Měiguo rén	ma?	Are you all Americans?
		lǎoshī		Are you all teachers?
		Rìběn rén		Are you all Japanese?
		Zhōngguo rén		Are you all Chinese?
		jīnglǐ		Are you all managers?
		Měiguo rén		Are you all Americans?

8.	Wǒmen bù dōu shi	Měiguo rén.	We are not all Americans.
		Jiā'nádà rén.	We are not all Canadians.
		xīn lǎoshī.	We are not all new teachers.
		xuésheng.	We are not all students.
		zǒngjīnglǐ.	We are not all general managers.
		tóngshì.	We are not all colleagues.
		Měiguo rén.	We are not all Americans.

9.	Wǒmen dōu bú shi	Měiguo rén.	None of us are Americans.
		Zhōngguo rén.	None of us are Chinese.
		Rìběn rén.	None of us are Japanese.
		lǎoshī.	None of us are teachers.
		jīnglǐ.	None of us are managers.
		háizi.	None of us are children.
		Měiguo rén.	None of us are Americans.

10.	Nèiwèi	tóngxué	yě shi Rìběn rén.	That classmate is also Japanese.
		lǎoshī		That teacher is also Japanese.
		Gāo Xiānsheng		That Mr. Gao is also Japanese.
		Kē Tàitai		That Mrs. Ke is also Japanese.
		Lín Xiáojie		That Miss Lin is also Japanese.
		tóngxué		That classmate is also Japanese.

11.	Nèiwèi	tóngxué jiào Wáng Jīngshēng?	Which student is called Wang Jingsheng?
	Zhèiwèi	.	This student is called Wang Jingsheng.
	Nèiwèi	.	That student is called Wang Jingsheng.
	Nèiwèi	?	Which student is called Wang Jingsheng?

- -

Unit 2, Part 2: Substitution Drills

Listen to the audio; after each prompt, say the new sentence using that substitution. Do each drill at least twice: first with the book open, then with the book closed. Each drill starts with a model sentence for you to repeat.

1. Zhè shi	wǒde	xīn tóngwū.	This is my new roommate.
	nǐde		This is your new roommate.
	tāde		This is her new roommate.
	Xiǎo Línde		This is Little Lin's new roommate.
	Lǎo Wángde		This is Old Wang's new roommate.
	wǒde		This is my new roommate.

2. Huānyíng nǐ dào	Zhōngguo	lái!	Welcome to China!
	wǒmende sùshè		Welcome to our dormitory!
	wǒmende shítáng		Welcome to our cafeteria!
	wǒmende túshūguǎn		Welcome to our library!
	Měiguo		Welcome to the United States!
	Rìběn		Welcome to Japan!
	Zhōngguo		Welcome to China!

3. Wǒ hěn gāoxing	rènshi nǐ.	I'm very happy to become acquainted with you.
	nǐ shi wǒde tóngwū.	I'm very happy that you are my roommate.
	nín shi wǒmende lǎoshī.	I'm very happy that you are our teacher.
	dào Zhōngguo qù.	I'm very happy to go to China.
	xuéxí Zhōngwén.	I'm very happy to study Chinese.
	dào Měiguo qù.	I'm very happy to go to the United States.
	rènshi nǐ.	I'm very happy to become acquainted with you.

4. Bié	zhèmme chēnghu wǒ!	Don't address me this way!
	wèn!	Don't ask!
	wèn ta!	Don't ask him!
	gāoxìng!	Don't be happy!
	bù gāoxìng!	Don't be unhappy!
	dào Zhōngguo qù!	Don't go to China!
	qù wǒmende sùshè!	Don't go to our dormitory!
	lái wǒmende shítáng!	Don't come to our dining hall!
	zhèmme chēnghu wǒ!	Don't address me this way!

5. Nǐ bú yào	zǒu!	Don't leave!
	qù!	Don't go!
	wèn!	Don't ask!
	lái!	Don't come!
	zuò!	Don't sit!
	zǒu!	Don't leave!

6. Háishi	jiào wǒ Xiǎo Chén	hǎole.	Why don't you just call me Little Chen.
	jiào wǒ Lǎo Luó		Why don't you just call me Old Luo.
	jiào tā Lín Tàitai		Why don't you just call her Mrs. Lin.
	dài nǐde tóngwū		Why don't you just bring your roommate.
	dài nǐde háizi		Why don't you just bring your kids.
	jiào wǒ Xiǎo Chén		Why don't you just call me Little Chen.

7. Wǒ yīnggāi zěmme chēnghu	nín?	How should I address you?
	nǐ?	How should I address you?
	tā?	How should I address him?
	nǐde tóngwū?	How should I address your roommate?
	nǐde bàba?	How should I address your father?
	nǐmende zǒngjīnglǐ?	How should I address your general manager?
	nín?	How should I address you?

8. Nà	shi shéi a?	Who is that?
Zhè		Who is this?
Tā		Who is she?
Tāmen		Who are they?
Nǐ		Who are you?
Nǐmen		Who are you all?
Wǒ		Who am I?
Wǒmen		Who are we?
Nà		Who is that?

Unit 2, Part 3: Substitution Drills

Listen to the audio; after each prompt, say the new sentence using that substitution. Do each drill at least twice: first with the book open, then with the book closed. Each drill starts with a model sentence for you to repeat.

1. Wǒ xìng	**Gāo.**	Nín guìxìng?	My name is Gao. What is your name?
	Wáng.		My name is Wang. What is your name?
	Lín.		My name is Lin. What is your name?
	Shī.		My name is Shi. What is your name?
	Wú.		My name is Wu. What is your name?
	Chén.		My name is Chen. What is your name?
	Gāo.		My name is Gao. What is your name?

2. Nín zài nèige	**dānwèi**	gōngzuò?	Which organization do you work at?
	gōngsī		Which company do you work at?
	dàxué		Which university do you work at?
	túshūguǎn		Which library do you work at?
	shítáng		Which cafeteria do you work at?
	dānwèi		Which organization do you work for?

3. Wǒ zài	**Xiānggǎng Zhōngwén Dàxué**	xuéxí.	I study at Chinese University of Hong Kong.
	sùshè		I study in the dormitory.
	túshūguǎn		I study at the library.
	shítáng		I study in the cafeteria.
	dānwèi		I study in my work unit.
	gōngsī		I study at the company.
	Xiānggǎng Zhōngwén Dàxué		I study at Chinese University of Hong Kong.

4. Xiǎo Wáng zài	**nèige**	dàshǐguǎn gōngzuò?	Which embassy does Little Wang work at?
	zhèige	.	Little Wang works at this embassy.
	nèige	.	Little Wang works at that embassy.
	nèige	?	Which embassy does Little Wang work at?

5. Tā bàba zài	**yìjiā**	gōngsī gōngzuò.	Her father works for a company.
	něijiā	?	Which company does her father work for?
	zhèijiā	.	Her father works for this company.
	nèijiā	.	Her father works for that company.
	yìjiā	.	Her father works for a company.

6. **Nèiwèi**	shi Mǎ Xiàozhǎng.		That is President Ma.
Zhèiwèi	.		This is President Ma.
Něiwèi	?		Which one is President Ma?
Nèiwèi	.		That is President Ma.

7. Tā shi nínde	**xiānsheng**	ba?	I suppose he is your husband?
	lǎoshī		I suppose he is your teacher?
	jīnglǐ		I suppose he is your manager?
	tàitai		I suppose she is your wife?
	tóngshì		I suppose she is your colleague?
	tóngwū		I suppose she is your roommate?
	tóngxué		I suppose she is your classmate?
	xiānsheng		I suppose he is your husband?

8. Nǐ hěn	**gāoxìng**	ba?	I suppose you must be happy?
	jǐnzhāng		I suppose you must be nervous?
	kùn		I suppose you must be sleepy?
	lèi		I suppose you must be tired?
	máng		I suppose you must be busy?
	gāoxìng		I suppose you must be happy?

9. Nǐmen yě	**gōngzuò**	ba?	I suppose you are also working?
	dài		I suppose you are also bringing some?
	rènshi		I suppose you are also acquainted?
	yǒu		I suppose you also have some?
	qù		I suppose you are also going?
	bàn		I suppose you are also doing it?
	gōngzuò		I suppose you are also working?

· ·

Unit 2, Part 4: Substitution Drills

Listen to the audio; after each prompt, say the new sentence using that substitution. Do each drill at least twice: first with the book open, then with the book closed. Each drill starts with a model sentence for you to repeat.

1. Duìbuqǐ, wǒ méi	dài míngpiàn.	Sorry, I didn't bring a name card.
	jièshao tā.	Sorry, I didn't introduce him.
	wèn nǐ.	Sorry, I didn't ask you.
	xièxie nǐ.	Sorry, I didn't thank you.
	dài míngpiàn.	Sorry, I didn't bring a name card.

2. Wǒ gēn Luó Xiáojie dōu bú	shi Yīngguo rén.	Miss Luo and I, neither one of us is English.
	lèi.	Miss Luo and I, neither one of us is tired.
	kùn.	Miss Luo and I, neither one of us is sleepy.
	shi Měiguo rén.	Miss Luo and I, neither one of us is American.
	shi Zhōngguo rén.	Miss Luo and I, neither one of us is Chinese.
	shi Yīngguo rén.	Miss Luo and I, neither one of us is English.

3. Wǒ gēn Luó Xiáojie dōu bù	gāoxìng.	Miss Luo and I, neither one of us is happy.
	lái.	Miss Luo and I, neither one of us is coming.
	gāo.	Miss Luo and I, neither one of us is tall.
	lǎo.	Miss Luo and I, neither one of us is old.
	máng.	Miss Luo and I, neither one of us is busy.
	zǒu.	Miss Luo and I, neither one of us is leaving.
	gāoxìng.	Miss Luo and I, neither one of us is happy.

4. Tāmen dōu méi	qù.	None of them went.
	lái.	None of them came.
	zuò.	None of them sat.
	zǒu.	None of them left.
	wèn.	None of them asked.
	dài.	None of them brought it.
	gōngzuò.	None of them worked.
	qù.	None of them went.

5. Zhè shi	Zhōng-Měi Màoyì Gōngsī	de Shī Xiáojie.	This is Miss Shi from the Sino-American Trading Company.
	Xiānggǎng Dàxué		This is Miss Shi from Hong Kong University.
	Rìběn Dàshǐguǎn		This is Miss Shi from the Japanese Embassy.
	túshūguǎn		This is Miss Shi from the library.
	Jiā'nádà Dàshǐguǎn		This is Miss Shi from the Canadian Embassy.
	Zhōng-Měi Màoyì Gōngsī		This is Miss Shi from the Sino-American Trading Company.

6. Nǐ rènshi nèiwèi	**tàitai**	**ma?**	Do you know that lady?
	xiānsheng		Do you know that gentleman?
	xiáojie		Do you know that young lady?
	nǚshì		Do you know that lady?
	lǎoshī		Do you know that teacher?
	xiàozhǎng		Do you know that president?
	tóngxué		Do you know that classmate?
	tàitai		Do you know that lady?

7. Nǐ dài bu dài	**míngpiàn?**	Are you bringing name cards?
	tóngxué?	Are you bringing classmates?
	tóngshì?	Are you bringing colleagues?
	nǐ xiānsheng?	Are you bringing your husband?
	nǐ tàitai?	Are you bringing your wife?
	nǐ māma?	Are you bringing your mother?
	nǐde háizi?	Are you bringing your children?
	Gāo Xiáojie?	Are you bringing Miss Gao?
	míngpiàn?	Are you bringing name cards?

8. Tāmen méi dōu	**qù.**	Not all of them went.
	zuò.	Not all of them sat.
	zǒu.	Not all of them left.
	wèn.	Not all of them asked.
	lái.	Not all of them came.
	qù.	Not all of them went.

. . . .

Unit 3, Part 1: Substitution Drills

Listen to the audio; after each prompt, say the new sentence using that substitution. Do each drill at least twice: first with the book open, then with the book closed. Each drill starts with a model sentence for you to repeat.

1. Tāmen bānshang yǒu	jǐge	tóngxué?	How many classmates are there in their class?
	yíge	.	There is one classmate in their class.
	liǎngge	.	There are two classmates in their class.
	sān'ge	.	There are three classmates in their class.
	sìge	.	There are four classmates in their class.
	wǔge	.	There are five classmates in their class.
	liùge	.	There are six classmates in their class.
	qíge	.	There are seven classmates in their class.
	báge	.	There are eight classmates in their class.
	jiǔge	.	There are nine classmates in their class.
	shíge	.	There are ten classmates in their class.
	jǐge	?	How many classmates are there in their class?

2. Bānshang	yǒu shíge rén.	In the class there are ten people.
Túshūguǎn		In the library there are ten people.
Sùshè		In the dormitory there are ten people.
Shítáng		In the dining hall there are ten people.
Gōngsī		In the company there are ten people.
Dānwèi		In the organization there are ten people.
Bānshang		In the class there are ten people.

3. Tāmen yǒu	jǐwèi	lǎoshī?	How many teachers do they have?
	yíwèi	.	They have one teacher.
	liǎngwèi	.	They have two teachers.
	sānwèi	.	They have three teachers.
	sìwèi	.	They have four teachers.
	wǔwèi	.	They have five teachers.
	liùwèi	.	They have six teachers.
	qíwèi	.	They have seven teachers.
	báwèi	.	They have eight teachers.
	jiǔwèi	.	They have nine teachers.
	shíwèi	.	They have ten teachers.
	jǐwèi	?	How many teachers do they have?

4. **Yígòng yǒu**

sānwèi.	In all, there are three of them.
sān'ge.	In all, there are three.
sān'ge rén.	In all, there are three people.
sān'ge nánshēng.	In all, there are three male students.
sān'ge nǚshēng.	In all, there are three female students.
sān'ge nánde.	In all, there are three men.
sān'ge nǚde.	In all, there are three women.
sān'ge háizi.	In all, there are three children.
sān'ge bān.	In all, there are three class sections.
sān'ge shítáng.	In all, there are three cafeterias.
sānwèi Zhào Xiáojie.	In all, there are three Miss Zhaos.
sānwèi nánlǎoshī.	In all, there are three male teachers.
sānwèi nǚlǎoshī.	In all, there are three female teachers.
sānwèi.	In all, there are three of them.

Unit 3, Part 2: Substitution Drills

Listen to the audio; after each prompt, say the new sentence using that substitution. Do each drill at least twice: first with the book open, then with the book closed. Each drill starts with a model sentence for you to repeat.

---

1. **Tā**	**duō dà niánji le?**		How old is she?
Tāde háizi			How old is her child?
Lǎo Gāo			How old is Old Gao?
Tāmen			How old are they?
Nèiwèi lǎoshī			How old is that teacher?
Wáng Xiáojie			How old is Ms. Wang?
Tā			How old is she?

---

2. **Nǐ mèimei**	**jǐsuì le?**		How old is your younger sister?
Nǐ dìdi			How old is your younger brother?
Zhèige háizi			How old is this child?
Nèige háizi			How old is that child?
Nǐde háizi			How old is your child?
Nǐ			How old are you?
Nǐmen			How old are you?
Nǐ mèimei			How old is your younger sister?

---

3. **Wǒ jīnnián**	**èrshi'èr**	**suì le.**	I'm twenty-two this year.
	shíliù		I'm sixteen this year.
	shíqī		I'm seventeen this year.
	shíbā		I'm eighteen this year.
	shíjiǔ		I'm nineteen this year.
	èrshí		I'm twenty this year.
	èrshiyī		I'm twenty-one this year.
	èrshi'èr		I'm twenty-two this year.

---

4. **Nǐ**	**xiángxiang**	**kàn.**	Try to think.
	wènwen		Try to ask.
	zuòzuo		Try to sit.
	cāicai		Try to guess.
	jiàojiao		Try to call (somebody's name).
	xiángxiang		Try to think.

---

5. **Zhè shi nǐ**	**mèimei**	**, duì bu duì?**	This is your younger sister, right?
	dìdi		This is your younger brother, right?
	gēge		This is your older brother, right?
	jiějie		This is your older sister, right?
	fùqin		This is your father, right?
	mǔqin		This is your mother, right?
	àiren		This is your spouse, right?
	mèimei		This is your younger sister, right?

6. Nǐ bié	kàn	, hǎo bu hǎo?	Don't look, O.K.?
	wèn		Don't ask, O.K.?
	lái		Don't come, O.K.?
	qù		Don't go, O.K.?
	zuò		Don't sit down, O.K.?
	zǒu		Don't leave, O.K.?
	cāi		Don't guess, O.K.?
	kàn		Don't look, O.K.?

7. Nǐ dìdi hěn	kě'ài!		Your younger brother is cute!
	gāo!		Your younger brother is tall!
	ǎi!		Your younger brother is short!
	dà!		Your younger brother is big!
	xiǎo!		Your younger brother is small!
	hǎo!		Your younger brother is good!
	gāoxìng!		Your younger brother is happy!
	máng!		Your younger brother is busy!
	kùn!		Your younger brother is sleepy!
	kě'ài!		Your younger brother is cute!

8. Tā xiàge yuè jiù	jiǔsuì	le.	She will be nine years old next month.
	èrshiyīsuì		She will be twenty-one years old next month.
	lái		She will come next month.
	bù lái		She will not come next month.
	yǒu		She will have it next month.
	méiyou		She will not have it next month.
	yǒu háizi		She will have a child next month.
	zǒu		She will leave next month.
	jiǔsuì		She will be nine years old next month.

Unit 3, Part 3: Substitution Drills

Listen to the audio; after each prompt, say the new sentence using that substitution. Do each drill at least twice: first with the book open, then with the book closed. Each drill starts with a model sentence for you to repeat.

1. Qǐng wèn,	zhèige	duōshǎo qián?	Excuse me, how much is this?
	zhèige bēibāo		Excuse me, how much is this backpack?
	nèige		Excuse me, how much is that?
	nèige bēibāo		Excuse me, how much is that backpack?
	bēizi		Excuse me, how much is that cup?
	gōngshìbāo		Excuse me, how much is that briefcase?
	yíge yuè		Excuse me, how much is it for a month?
	liǎngge yuè		Excuse me, how much is it for two months?
	zhèige		Excuse me, how much is this?

2. Yò, tài	guì	le.	Gosh, that's too expensive.
	dà		Gosh, that's too big.
	xiǎo		Gosh, that's too small.
	cháng		Gosh, that's too long.
	nán		Gosh, that's too hard.
	guì		Gosh, that's too expensive.

3. Nèige zhǐ yào	sānkuài wǔ.	That is only three dollars and fifty cents.
	yìfēn qián.	That is only one cent.
	liùkuài wǔ.	That is only six dollars and fifty cents.
	shíkuài qián.	That is only ten dollars.
	jiǔqiān jiǔbǎi jiǔshíjiǔkuài.	That is only nine thousand nine hundred and ninety-nine dollars.
	qīkuài sì.	That is only seven dollars and forty cents.
	sānkuài wǔ.	That is only three dollars and fifty cents.

4. Wǒ kànkan,	xíng bu xíng?	Let me see, O.K.?
	xíng ma?	Let me see, O.K.?
	hǎo bu hǎo?	Let me see, O.K.?
	hǎo ma?	Let me see, O.K.?
	xíng bu xíng?	Let me see, O.K.?

5. Qǐng nǐ	kànkan.	Please take a look.
	wènwen.	Please ask.
	zuòzuo.	Please sit down.
	xiángxiang.	Please think about it.
	cāicai.	Please guess.
	kànkan.	Please take a look.

6. Nín	kàn	ba.	Why don't you look.
	cāi		Why don't you guess.
	wèn		Why don't you ask.
	mǎi		Why don't you buy it.
	mài		Why don't you sell it.
	zuò		Why don't you sit.
	zǒu		Why don't you leave.
	lái		Why don't you come.
	qù		Why don't you go.
	kàn		Why don't you look.

7. Wǒmen	zǒu	ba.	Let's leave.
	huí sùshè		Let's return to the dormitory.
	qù túshūguǎn		Let's go to the library.
	yě dài míngpiàn		Let's also bring name cards.
	yě xuéxí Zhōngwén		Let's also study Chinese.
	yě jiào tā Xiǎo Mǎ		Let's also call him Little Ma.
	yě mǎi yíge		Let's also buy one.
	zǒu		Let's leave.

8. Wǒ méi dài	míngpiàn.	I didn't bring name cards.
	qián.	I didn't bring money.
	gōngzuò.	I didn't bring work.
	bēizi.	I didn't bring a cup.
	dàizi.	I didn't bring a bag.
	bēibāo.	I didn't bring a backpack.
	gōngshìbāo.	I didn't bring a briefcase.
	míngpiàn.	I didn't bring name cards.

· ·

Unit 3, Part 4: Substitution Drills

Listen to the audio; after each prompt, say the new sentence using that substitution. Do each drill at least twice: first with the book open, then with the book closed. Each drill starts with a model sentence for you to repeat.

1. Xià yítàng dào	**Tiānjīn**	de huǒchē jǐdiǎn kāi?	When does the next train for Tianjin depart?
	Yīngguo		When does the next train for England depart?
	Fǎguo		When does the next train for France depart?
	Déguo		When does the next train for Germany depart?
	Xībānyá		When does the next train for Spain depart?
	Měiguo		When does the next train for the U.S. depart?
	Jiā'nádà		When does the next train for Canada depart?
	Zhōngguo		When does the next train for China depart?
	Tiānjīn		When does the next train for Tianjin depart?

2. **Xià yítàng dào Tiānjīn**	de huǒchē jǐdiǎn kāi?	When does the next train for Tianjin depart?
Bādiǎn èrshí dào Tiānjīn		When does the train that arrives in Tianjin at 8:20 depart?
Shí'èrdiǎn dào Xīnjiāpō		When does the train that arrives in Singapore at 12:00 depart?
Wǒ gēn Bái Tàitai zuò		When does the train that Mrs. Bai and I are taking depart?
Tāmen yīnggāi zuò		When does the train that they're supposed to take depart?
Lǎo Chén děi zuò		When does the train that Old Chen must take depart?
Xià yítàng dào Tiānjīn		When does the next train for Tianjin depart?

3. Tā	**yīdiǎn**	èrshí dào.	She arrives at 1:20.
	liǎngdiǎn		She arrives at 2:20.
	sāndiǎn		She arrives at 3:20.
	sìdiǎn		She arrives at 4:20.
	wǔdiǎn		She arrives at 5:20.
	liùdiǎn		She arrives at 6:20.
	qīdiǎn		She arrives at 7:20.
	bādiǎn		She arrives at 8:20.
	jiǔdiǎn		She arrives at 9:20.
	shídiǎn		She arrives at 10:20.
	shíyīdiǎn		She arrives at 11:20.
	shí'èrdiǎn		She arrives at 12:20.
	yīdiǎn		She arrives at 1:20.

4. Jiǔdiǎn	èrshí.	9:20.
	bàn.	9:30.
	sānkè.	9:45.
	wǔshí.	9:50.
	wǔfēn.	9:05.
	shífēn.	9:10.
	yíkè.	9:15.
	èrshí.	9:20.

5. Kǒngpà nín	láibujíle.	I'm afraid you're not going to make it.
	gǎocuòle.	I'm afraid you got it wrong.
	lèile.	I'm afraid you're tired.
	kùnle.	I'm afraid you've gotten sleepy.
	děi zǒule.	I'm afraid you have to go now.
	láibujíle.	I'm afraid you're not going to make it.

6. Nà, wǒ jiù zuò	shídiǎn bàn de.	In that case, I'll take the 10:30 one.
	liùdiǎn yíkè	In that case, I'll take the 6:15 one.
	qīdiǎn sānkè	In that case, I'll take the 7:45 one.
	bādiǎn wǔfēn	In that case, I'll take the 8:05 one.
	jiǔdiǎn èrshí	In that case, I'll take the 9:20 one.
	wǔdiǎn bàn	In that case, I'll take the 5:30 one.
	sìdiǎn yíkè	In that case, I'll take the 4:15 one.
	shídiǎn bàn	In that case, I'll take the 10:30 one.

7. Dào	Tiānjīn yào duō cháng shíjiān?	How long does it take to get to Tianjin?
	Fǎguo	How long does it take to get to France?
	túshūguǎn	How long does it take to get to the library?
	shítáng	How long does it take to get to the cafeteria?
	sùshè	How long does it take to get to the dormitory?
	Déguo	How long does it take to get to Germany?
	Tiānjīn	How long does it take to get to Tianjin?

8. Chàbuduō yào	liǎngge bàn zhōngtóu.	It takes about two and a half hours.
	bàn'ge	It takes about half an hour.
	yíge bàn	It takes about one and a half hours.
	sān'ge bàn	It takes about three and a half hours.
	yíge	It takes about one hour.
	qīge bàn	It takes about seven and a half hours.
	liǎngge bàn	It takes about two and a half hours.

· ·

Unit 4, Part 1: Substitution Drills

Listen to the audio; after each prompt, say the new sentence using that substitution. Do each drill at least twice: first with the book open, then with the book closed. Each drill starts with a model sentence for you to repeat.

1. Qǐng wèn, **yǔyán shíyànshì** jǐdiǎn zhōng kāimén? | Excuse me, what time does the language lab open?

túshūguǎn	Excuse me, what time does the library open?
shítáng	Excuse me, what time does the cafeteria open?
dàshǐguǎn	Excuse me, what time does the embassy open?
màoyì gōngsī	Excuse me, what time does the trading company open?
shíyànshì	Excuse me, what time does the laboratory open?
yǔyán shíyànshì	Excuse me, what time does the language lab open?

2. Qǐng wèn, **yǔyán shíyànshì** jǐdiǎn zhōng guānmén? | Excuse me, what time does the language lab close?

túshūguǎn	Excuse me, what time does the library close?
shítáng	Excuse me, what time does the cafeteria close?
dàshǐguǎn	Excuse me, what time does the embassy close?
màoyì gōngsī	Excuse me, what time does the trading company close?
shíyànshì	Excuse me, what time does the laboratory close?
yǔyán shíyànshì	Excuse me, what time does the language lab close?

3. Měitiān zǎoshang | **bādiǎn** | kāimén. | It opens at 8:00 A.M. every day.

	qīdiǎn bàn	It opens at 7:30 A.M. every day.
	shídiǎn yíkè	It opens at 10:15 A.M. every day.
	liùdiǎn bàn	It opens at 6:30 A.M. every day.
	jiǔdiǎn sānkè	It opens at 9:45 A.M. every day.
	shídiǎn wǔfēn	It opens at 10:05 A.M. every day.
	bādiǎn	It opens at 8:00 A.M. every day.

4. Wǎnshang | **jiǔdiǎn bàn** | guānmén. | It closes at 9:30 P.M.

	shídiǎn bàn	It closes at 10:30 P.M.
	bādiǎn yíkè	It closes at 8:15 P.M.
	liùdiǎn sānkè	It closes at 6:45 P.M.
	qīdiǎn	It closes at 7:00 P.M.
	jiǔdiǎn bàn	It closes at 9:30 P.M.

5. **Xīngqīliù**   kāi bu kāi?   Is it open on Saturday?
   Xīngqīyī   Is it open on Monday?
   Xīngqī'èr   Is it open on Tuesday?
   Xīngqīsān   Is it open on Wednesday?
   Xīngqīsì   Is it open on Thursday?
   Xīngqīwǔ   Is it open on Friday?
   Xīngqītiān   Is it open on Sunday?
   Xīngqīrì   Is it open on Sunday?
   Xīngqīliù   Is it open on Saturday?

6. **Lǐbàiliù**   kāi bàntiān.   It's open half-days on Saturday.
   Lǐbàiyī   It's open half-days on Monday.
   Lǐbài'èr   It's open half-days on Tuesday.
   Lǐbàisān   It's open half-days on Wednesday.
   Lǐbàisì   It's open half-days on Thursday.
   Lǐbàiwǔ   It's open half-days on Friday.
   Lǐbàitiān   It's open half-days on Sunday.
   Lǐbàirì   It's open half-days on Sunday.
   Lǐbàiliù   It's open half-days on Saturday.

7. **Xīngqītiān**   xiūxi.   He rests on Sundays.
   Zǎoshang   It's closed in the morning.
   Wǎnshang   It's closed in the evening.
   Shàngwǔ   It's closed mornings.
   Xiàwǔ   It's closed afternoons.
   Shàngge xīngqī   It was closed last week.
   Zhèige xīngqī   It's closed this week.
   Xiàge xīngqī   It's closed next week.
   Píngcháng   It's ordinarily closed.
   Měitiān dōu   It's closed every day.
   Xīngqītiān   He rests on Sundays.

8. Wǒ píngcháng zǎoshang **qīdiǎn**   qǐchuáng. I usually get up from bed at 7:00 A.M.
            wǔdiǎn bàn   I usually get up from bed at 5:30 A.M.
            liùdiǎn yíkè   I usually get up from bed at 6:15 A.M.
            bādiǎn bàn   I usually get up from bed at 8:30 A.M.
            jiǔdiǎn sānkè   I usually get up from bed at 9:45 A.M.
            qīdiǎn èrshí   I usually get up from bed at 7:20 A.M.
            qīdiǎn   I usually get up from bed at 7:00 A.M.

9.	Wǒ píngcháng	shíyīdiǎn zhōng	shuìjiào.	I usually go to bed at 11:00.
		liǎngdiǎn bàn		I usually go to bed at 2:30.
		shídiǎn yíkè		I usually go to bed at 10:15.
		shí'èrdiǎn sānkè		I usually go to bed at 12:45.
		sāndiǎn zhōng		I usually go to bed at 3:00.
		yīdiǎn bàn		I usually go to bed at 1:30.
		liǎngdiǎn yíkè		I usually go to bed at 2:15.
		shíyīdiǎn		I usually go to bed at 11:00.

10.	Wǒ píngcháng měitiān shuì	qíge	zhōngtóu.	I usually sleep for seven hours every day.
		báge		I usually sleep for eight hours every day.
		liùge bàn		I usually sleep for six and a half hours every day.
		sìge		I usually sleep for four hours every day.
		wǔge bàn		I usually sleep for five and a half hours every day.
		shí'èrge		I usually sleep for twelve hours every day.
		shíge		I usually sleep for ten hours every day.
		qíge		I usually sleep for seven hours every day.

Unit 4, Part 2: Substitution Drills

Listen to the audio; after each prompt, say the new sentence using that substitution. Do each drill at least twice: first with the book open, then with the book closed. Each drill starts with a model sentence for you to repeat.

1. **Nǐ**	jiào shémme míngzi?	What is your name?
Tā		What is her name?
Nǐ àiren		What is your spouse's name?
Nǐde háizi		What is your child's name?
Nǐde tóngwū		What is your roommate's name?
Nǐde tóngxué		What is your classmate's name?
Nèiwèi tóngshì		What is that colleague's name?
Nǐ		What is your name?

2. **Nǐ**	shi něinián chūshēngde?	In what year were you born?
Tā		In what year was she born?
Gāo Xiānsheng		In what year was Mr. Gao born?
Bái Xiáojie		In what year was Ms. Bai born?
Lǎo Wáng		In what year was Old Wang born?
Xiǎo Lín		In what year was Little Lin born?
Tāmen		In what year were they born?
Chén Tàitai		In what year was Mrs. Chen born?
Nǐ		In what year were you born?

3. Wǒ shi	**yī-jiǔ-qī-jiǔ-nián** chūshēngde.	I was born in 1979.
	yī-jiǔ-bā-líng-nián	I was born in 1980.
	yī-jiǔ-bā-yī-nián	I was born in 1981.
	yī-jiǔ-bā-èr-nián	I was born in 1982.
	yī-jiǔ-jiǔ-sān-nián	I was born in 1993.
	yī-jiǔ-jiǔ-sì-nián	I was born in 1994.
	yī-jiǔ-jiǔ-wǔ-nián	I was born in 1995.
	yī-jiǔ-qī-jiǔ-nián	I was born in 1979.

4. Wǒde shēngrì shi	**sìyuè shísānhào.**	My birthday is April 13th.
	shíyuè yīhào.	My birthday is October 1st.
	sānyuè èrshibāhào.	My birthday is March 28th.
	jiǔyuè sìhào.	My birthday is September 4th.
	liùyuè èrshihào.	My birthday is June 20th
	wǔyuè sānhào.	My birthday is May 3rd.
	yīyuè sānshihào.	My birthday is January 30th.
	sìyuè shísānhào.	My birthday is April 13th.

5. Wénhuà Lù	sìhào		4 Culture Road
	sānbǎi èrshisānhào		323 Culture Road
	bābǎi líng wǔhào		805 Culture Road
	shísānhào		13 Culture Road
	sānshihào		30 Culture Road
	jiǔhào		9 Culture Road
	sìbǎi wǔshiwǔhào		455 Culture Road
	sìhào		4 Culture Road

6. Hépíng Dōng Lù	yī	duàn sìhào	Number 4, Heping East Road Section One
	èr		Number 4, Heping East Road Section Two
	sān		Number 4, Heping East Road Section Three
	sì		Number 4, Heping East Road Section Four
	wǔ		Number 4, Heping East Road Section Five
	liù		Number 4, Heping East Road Section Six
	qī		Number 4, Heping East Road Section Seven
	yī		Number 4, Heping East Road Section One

7. Tiānjīn Lù	èrxiàng	qīhào	Number 7, Lane 2, Tianjin Road
	yīxiàng		Number 7, Lane 1, Tianjin Road
	sānxiàng		Number 7, Lane 3, Tianjin Road
	sìxiàng		Number 7, Lane 4, Tianjin Road
	wǔxiàng		Number 7, Lane 5, Tianjin Road
	liùxiàng		Number 7, Lane 6, Tianjin Road
	qīxiàng		Number 7, Lane 7, Tianjin Road
	èrxiàng		Number 7, Lane 2, Tianjin Road

8. Tā yào qù	jǐlóu?	What floor does she want to go to?
	yìlóu.	She wants to go to the first floor.
	èrlóu.	She wants to go to the second floor.
	sānlóu.	She wants to go to the third floor.
	sìlóu.	She wants to go to the fourth floor.
	wǔlóu.	She wants to go to the fifth floor.
	liùlóu.	She wants to go to the sixth floor.
	qīlóu.	She wants to go to the seventh floor.
	jǐlóu?	What floor does she want to go to?

9.	Qǐng	nǐ	děng yíxià.	Could you wait a moment, please?
		tā		Could she wait a moment, please?
		tāmen		Could they wait a moment, please?
		Zhào Xiānsheng		Could Mr. Zhao wait a moment, please?
		Xiè Tàitai		Could Mrs. Xie wait a moment, please?
		Wáng Xiáojie		Could Miss Wang wait a moment, please?
		Lǎo Zhāng		Could Old Zhang wait a moment, please?
		Xiǎo Mǎ		Could Little Ma wait a moment, please?
		nǐ		Could you wait a moment, please?

10.	Jīntiān	jǐyuè jǐhào?	What is today's date?
	Míngtiān		What is tomorrow's date?
	Zuótiān		What was yesterday's date?
	Jīnnián		Which month and which day this year?
	Míngnián		Which month and which day next year?
	Qùnián		Which month and which day last year?
	Nǐde shēngrì		When is your birthday?
	Jīntiān		What is today's date?

11.	Jīnnián	shi něinián?	What year is this year?
	Míngnián		What year will it be next year?
	Qùnián		What year was it last year?
	Jīnnián		What year is this year?

. . . .

Unit 4, Part 3: Substitution Drills

Listen to the audio; after each prompt, say the new sentence using that substitution. Do each drill at least twice: first with the book open, then with the book closed. Each drill starts with a model sentence for you to repeat.

1. Zhè shi tā dì	jǐ	cì dào Zhōngguo lái?	How many times has he been to China?
	yī	.	This is his first time in China.
	èr	.	This is his second time in China.
	sān	.	This is his third time in China.
	sì	.	This is his fourth time in China.
	wǔ	.	This is his fifth time in China.
	liù	.	This is his sixth time in China.
	qī	.	This is his seventh time in China.
	bā	.	This is his eighth time in China.
	jiǔ	.	This is his ninth time in China.
	jǐ	?	How many times has he been to China?

2. Zhè shi wǒ dì	èr	cì lái.	This is my second time here.
	yī		This is my first time here.
	sān		This is my third time here.
	sì		This is my fourth time here.
	wǔ		This is my fifth time here.
	liù		This is my sixth time here.
	qī		This is my seventh time here.
	bā		This is my eighth time here.
	jiǔ		This is my ninth time here.
	èr		This is my second time here.

3. Dì	yí	ge rén shi shéi?	Who was the first person?
	èr		Who was the second person?
	sān		Who was the third person?
	sì		Who was the fourth person?
	wǔ		Who was the fifth person?
	liù		Who was the sixth person?
	qī		Who was the seventh person?
	bā		Who was the eighth person?
	jiǔ		Who was the ninth person?
	shí		Who was the tenth person?
	yí		Who was the first person?

4. Yǒu yìsi, dì	èr	wèi lǎoshī yě xìng Wáng!	Interesting, the 2nd teacher's surname was also Wang!
	sān		Interesting, the 3rd teacher's surname was also Wang!
	sì		Interesting, the 4th teacher's surname was also Wang!
	wǔ		Interesting, the 5th teacher's surname was also Wang!
	liù		Interesting, the 6th teacher's surname was also Wang!
	qī		Interesting, the 7th teacher's surname was also Wang!
	bā		Interesting, the 8th teacher's surname was also Wang!
	èr		Interesting, the 2nd teacher's surname was also Wang!

5. Wǒ	lái	guo.	I've been here before.
	qù		I've been there before.
	wèn		I've asked before.
	mǎi		I've bought them before.
	mài		I've sold them before.
	lái		I've been here before.

6. Tā láiguo	yí	cì.	She has been here once.
	liǎng	.	She has been here twice.
	sān	.	She has been here three times.
	sì	.	She has been here four times.
	wǔ	.	She has been here five times.
	liù	.	She has been here six times.
	qī	.	She has been here seven times.
	bā	.	She has been here eight times.
	jiǔ	.	She has been here nine times.
	shí	.	She has been here ten times
	jǐ	?	How many times has she been here?
	yí	.	She has been here once.

7. Lǎo Zhào méi	zuò	guo.	Old Zhao has never taken one (e.g., a train) before.
	mǎi		Old Zhao has never bought one before.
	mài		Old Zhao has never sold one before.
	shuō		Old Zhao has never said it before.
	zuò		Old Zhao has never taken one before.

8. Tā zhèicì yào zhù	duō jiǔ?	How long will he stay this time?
	liǎngtiān.	He will stay for two days this time.
	liǎngge xīngqī.	He will stay for two weeks this time.
	liǎngge yuè.	He will stay for two months this time.
	liǎngnián.	He will stay for two years this time.
	bàn'ge yuè.	He will stay for half a month this time.
	yíge bàn yuè.	He will stay for one and a half months this time.
	duō jiǔ?	How long will he stay this time?

9. Wǒ míngtiān huí
	guó.	I'll return to my native country tomorrow.
	jiā.	I'll go home tomorrow.
	sùshè.	I'll return to my dorm tomorrow.
	xuéxiào.	I'll return to school tomorrow.
	guó.	I'll return to my native country tomorrow.

10. Nǐ zhù
něige	fángjiān?	In which room are you staying?
jǐhào		What is the number of the room in which you are staying?
shéide		Whose room are you staying in?
něige		In which room are you staying?

11. Tā zhù
sān líng liù.	She is staying in 306.
èr jiǔ bā.	She is staying in 298.
sùshè.	She is staying in the dormitory.
wǒ jiā.	She is staying in my home.
něige fángjiān?	Which room is she staying in?
wǒde fángjiān.	She is staying in my room.
nǎr?	Where is she staying?
sān líng liù.	She is staying in 306.

12. Tā xiān
shuōle	shémme? Ránhòu	shuōle	shémme?	What did he say first? What did he say then?
zuòle		zuòle		What did he do first? What did he do then?
wènle		wènle		What did he ask first? What did he ask then?
mǎile		mǎile		What did he buy first? What did he buy then?
kànle		kànle		What did he look at first? What did he look at then?
shuōle		shuōle		What did he say first? What did he say then?

13. Nǐ shì bu shi
qiántiān	láiguo wǒ jiā?	Did you come to my house the day before yesterday?
zuótiān		Did you come to my house yesterday?
jīntiān shàngwǔ		Did you come to my house this morning?
qiánnián		Did you come to my house the year before last?
qùnián		Did you come to my house last year?
jīnnián èryuè		Did you come to my house February of this year?
qiántiān		Did you come to my house the day before yesterday?

14. Bái Xiānsheng shuō tā

jīnnián	bù huíguó.	Mr. Bai says he won't return to his country this year.
míngnián		Mr. Bai says he won't return to his country next year.
hòunián		Mr. Bai says he won't return to his country the year after next.
xiàge yuè		Mr. Bai says he won't return to his country next month.
xiàge xīngqī		Mr. Bai says he won't return to his country next week.
míngtiān		Mr. Bai says he won't return to his country tomorrow.
hòutiān		Mr. Bai says he won't return to his country the day after tomorrow.
jīnnián		Mr. Bai says he won't return to his country this year.

Unit 4, Part 4: Substitution Drills

Listen to the audio; after each prompt, say the new sentence using that substitution. Do each drill at least twice: first with the book open, then with the book closed. Each drill starts with a model sentence for you to repeat.

1. Qǐng wèn,	**Zhōngguo**	yǒu duōshǎo rén?	Excuse me, how many people are there in China?
	Měiguo		Excuse me, how many people are there in the United States?
	Fǎguo		Excuse me, how many people are there in France?
	Déguo		Excuse me, how many people are there in Germany?
	Rìběn		Excuse me, how many people are there in Japan?
	Yīngguo		Excuse me, how many people are there in England?
	Zhōngguo		Excuse me, how many people are there in China?

2. Chàbuduō yǒu	**shísānyì**	rén.	There are about 1.3 billion people.
	liùqiān		There are about 6,000 people.
	sānwàn		There are about 30,000 people.
	èrshiwǔwàn		There are about 250,000 people.
	yībǎiwàn		There are about 1 million people.
	liǎngqiānwàn		There are about 20 million people.
	yíyì		There are about 100 million people.
	shísānyì		There are about 1.3 billion people.

3. **Nánjīng**	de rénkǒu bǐjiào shǎo.	The population of Nanjing is smaller.
Tiānjīn		The population of Tianjin is smaller.
Běijīng		The population of Beijing is smaller.
Yīngguo		The population of England is smaller.
Xīnjiāpō		The population of Singapore is smaller.
Nánjīng		The population of Nanjing is smaller.

4. Běijīng Dōng Lù bǐjiào	**hǎo.**	Beijing East Road is better.
	guì.	Beijing East Road is more expensive.
	piányi.	Beijing East Road is cheaper.
	dà.	Beijing East Road is bigger.
	xiǎo.	Beijing East Road is smaller.
	duō.	Beijing East Road has more.
	shǎo.	Beijing East Road has less.
	hǎo.	Beijing East Road is better.

5. Hǎoxiàng	**Nánjīng zhǐ yǒu wǔbǎiwàn rén.**	Apparently, Nanjing only has 5 million people.
	měitiān dōu yǒu Zhōngwén kè.	Apparently, we have Chinese class every day.
	zhè shi tā dìyícì dào Zhōngguo.	Apparently, this is her first time in China.
	yǔyán shíyànshì bù kāimén.	Apparently, the language lab is not open.
	tāmen méi dài míngpiàn.	Apparently, they didn't bring name cards.
	Nánjīng zhǐ yǒu wǔbǎiwàn rén.	Apparently, Nanjing only has 5 million people.

6. Xiǎo Sūn chángcháng	**táokè.**	Little Sun often skips class.
	chídào.	Little Sun is often late.
	bù lái.	Little Sun often doesn't come.
	bù lái shàngkè.	Little Sun often doesn't come to class.
	táokè.	Little Sun often skips class.

For the remaining pages of Substitution Drills
(**Unit 5, Part 1** through **Unit 10, Part 4**),
please refer to the disc.

3. Transformation and Response Drills
Unit 1, Part 1: Transformation and Response Drills

1. Add the final particle **a** to the following greetings and questions to make them softer and more colloquial.

Nǐ hǎo!
"How are you?"

Nǐ hǎo a?
"How are you?"

Wáng Jīngshēng, nǐ hǎo!
"Wang Jingsheng, how are you?"

Wáng Jīngshēng, nǐ hǎo a!
"Wang Jingsheng, how are you?"

Nǐ dào nǎr qù?
"Where are you going?"

Nǐ dào nǎr qù a?
"Where are you going?"

Kē Léi'ēn dào nǎr qù bàn shì?
"Where is Ke Leien going to take care of things?"

Kē Léi'ēn dào nǎr qù bàn shì a?
"Where is Ke Leien going to take care of things?"

2. Use **ne** to abbreviate the question about the second person.

Wǒ huí sùshè. Nǐ dào nǎr qù?
"I'm going back to the dormitory.
Where are you going?"

Wǒ huí sùshè. Nǐ ne?
"I'm going back to the dormitory.
How about you?"

Wǒ qù bàn yìdiǎnr shì. Nǐ dào nǎr qù?
"I'm going to go take care of some stuff. Where are you going?"

Wǒ qù bàn yìdiǎnr shì. Nǐ ne?
"I'm going to go take care of some stuff. And you?"

Wǒ qù shítáng. Nǐ dào nǎr qù?
"I'm going to the cafeteria. Where are you going?"

Wǒ qù shítáng. Nǐ ne?
"I'm going to the cafeteria. And how about you?"

Wǒ qù túshūguǎn. Nǐ dào nǎr qù?
"I'm going to the library. Where are you going?"

Wǒ qù túshūguǎn. Nǐ ne?
"I'm going to the library. And you?"

3. You will hear a statement about somebody who is going to do something. Repeat the statement and, using the adverb **yě** "also, too," add a comment to the effect that you are going to do the same thing as the person being talked about.

Kē Léi'ēn huí sùshè.
"Ke Leien is returning to the dormitory."

Kē Léi'ēn huí sùshè, wǒ yě huí sùshè.
"Ke Leien is returning to the dormitory, and I'm returning to the dormitory, too."

Wáng Jīngshēng qù shítáng.
"Wang Jingsheng is going to the cafeteria."

Wáng Jīngshēng qù shítáng, wǒ yě qù shítáng.
"Wang Jingsheng is going to the cafeteria, and I'm going to the cafeteria, too."

Nǐ qù túshūguǎn.
"You're going to the library."

Nǐ qù túshūguǎn, wǒ yě qù túshūguǎn.
"You're going to the library, and I'm going to the library, too."

Nǐ qù bàn yìdiǎnr shì.
"You're going to go take care of some things."

Nǐ qù bàn yìdiǎnr shì, wǒ yě qù bàn yìdiǎnr shì.
"You're going to go take care of some things, and I'm going to go take care of some things, too."

. . . .

Unit 1, Part 2: Transformation and Response Drills

1. Add **dōu** to each sentence.

Wǒ bàba, māma hěn máng.
"My father and mother are busy."

Wǒ bàba, māma dōu hěn máng.
"My father and mother are both busy."

Wǒ àiren, háizi qù túshūguǎn.
"My spouse and children go to the library."

Wǒ àiren, háizi dōu qù túshūguǎn.
"My spouse and children all go to the library."

Tāmen xiān zǒule.
"They left early."

Tāmen dōu xiān zǒule.
"They all left early."

Nǐ bàba, māma hěn lèi.
"Your father and mother are tired."

Nǐ bàba, māma dōu hěn lèi.
"Your father and mother are both tired."

2. Change the following statements into questions by adding the question particle **ma**.

Tāmen hěn máng.
"They are busy."

Tāmen hěn máng ma?
"Are they very busy?"

Nǐ lèile.
"You've gotten tired."

Nǐ lèile ma?
"Have you gotten tired?"

Tāmen qù túshūguǎn.
"They're going to the library."

Tāmen qù túshūguǎn ma?
"Are they going to the library?"

Tā huí sùshè.
"She's going back to the dormitory."

Tā huí sùshè ma?
"Is she going back to the dormitory?"

Wǒ àiren xiān zǒule.
"My spouse left already."

Wǒ àiren xiān zǒule ma?
"Did my spouse leave already?"

Tā hái hǎo.
"He's O.K."

Tā hái hǎo ma?
"Is he O.K.?"

3. Create stative verb sentences with **hěn** using the subjects and stative verbs given you.

Nǐmen, lèi.
"You (plural), tired."

Nǐmen hěn lèi.
"You are very tired."

Tā, máng.
"She, busy."

Tā hěn máng.
"She is very busy."

Wǒ, hǎo.
"I, good."

Wǒ hěn hǎo.
"I am doing very well."

Nǐ, máng.
"You, busy."

Nǐ hěn máng.
"You are very busy."

Tāmen, lèi.
"They, tired."

Tāmen hěn lèi.
"They are very tired."

4. Change the pronoun subject **tā** to the plural by adding **-men**.

Tā qù túshūguǎn.
"He's going to the library."

Tāmen qù túshūguǎn.
"They're going to the library."

Tā huí sùshè.
"She's going back to the dormitory."

Tāmen huí sùshè.
"They're going back to the dormitory."

Tā hěn máng.
"He is very busy."

Tāmen hěn máng.
"They are very busy."

Tā xiān zǒule.
"She left earlier."

Tāmen xiān zǒule.
"They left earlier."

· ·

Unit 1, Part 3: Transformation and Response Drills

1. Change the following from the pattern NOUN + STATIVE VERB to the pattern STATIVE VERB USED AS AN ADJECTIVE + NOUN.

Gōngzuò hǎo.
"The job is good."

hǎo gōngzuò
"good job"

Háizi xiǎo.
"The child is little."

xiǎo háizi
"little child"

Bàba hǎo.
"Father is good."

hǎo bàba
"good father"

Shítáng hǎo.
"The cafeteria is good."

hǎo shítáng
"good cafeteria"

Shìr xiǎo.
"The matter is small."

xiǎo shìr
"small matter"

Yàngzi lǎo.
"The appearance is old."

lǎo yàngzi
"old appearance, old way"

2. Transform the following verbs to the negative with **bù**. Remember that before syllables in Tone Four, **bù** changes from Tone Four to Tone Two to become **bú**.

máng
"busy"

bù máng
"not busy"

jǐnzhāng
"nervous"

bù jǐnzhāng
"not nervous"

lèi
"tired"

bú lèi
"not tired"

xiǎo
"little"

bù xiǎo
"not little"

lǎo
"old"

bù lǎo
"not old"

kùn
"sleepy"

bú kùn
"not sleepy"

nán
"hard"

bù nán
"not hard"

róngyi
"easy"

bù róngyi
"not easy"

qù
"go"

bú qù
"not go"

3. Change the following sentences into the negative by adding **bù** or **bú**.

Wǒ huí sùshè.
"I'm going back to the dormitory."

Wǒ bù huí sùshè.
"I'm not going back to the dormitory."

Tāmen hǎo ma?
"Are they well?"

Tāmen bù hǎo ma?
"Are they not well?"

Nǐ háizi lèi ma?
"Is your child tired?"

Nǐ háizi bú lèi ma?
"Is your child not tired?"

Nǐmen hěn máng.
"You are very busy."

Nǐmen bù hěn máng.
"You are not very busy."

Bàba qù gōngzuò.
"Father goes to work."

Bàba bú qù gōngzuò.
"Father does not go to work."

Xuéxí Zhōngwén nán ma?
"Is learning Chinese hard?"

Xuéxí Zhōngwén bù nán ma?
"Is learning Chinese not hard?"

4. Change the following statements into questions by using the positive-negative question pattern.

Tā qù.
"She is going."

Tā qù bu qù?
"Is she going or not?"

Nǐ hěn kùn.
"You are sleepy."

Nǐ kùn bu kùn?
"Are you sleepy or not?"

Tāmen hěn máng.
"They are busy."

Tāmen máng bu máng?
"Are they busy or not?"

Bàba hěn lèi.
"Dad is tired."

Bàba lèi bu lèi?
"Is Dad tired or not?"

Māma hěn gāo.
"Mom is tall."

Māma gāo bu gāo?
"Is Mom tall or not?"

Tā hěn hǎo.
"He is good."

Tā hǎo bu hǎo?
"Is he good or not?"

Zhōngwén hěn nán.
"Chinese is hard."

Zhōngwén nán bu nán?
"Is Chinese hard or not?"

5. Convert the following **ma** questions into positive-negative questions.

Nǐ zuìjìn hǎo ma?
"Have you been well recently?"

Nǐ zuìjìn hǎo bu hǎo?
"Have you been well recently or not?"

Tā qù túshūguǎn ma?
"Does he go to the library?"

Tā qù bu qù túshūguǎn?
"Does he go to the library or not?"

Zhōngwén róngyi ma?
"Is Chinese easy?"

Zhōngwén róngyi bu róngyi?
"Is Chinese easy or not?"

Nǐ gōngzuò jǐnzhāng ma?
"Is your work intense?"

Nǐ gōngzuò jǐnzhāng bu jǐnzhāng?
"Is your work intense or not?"

Tā àiren ǎi ma?
"Is her spouse short?"

Tā àiren ǎi bu ǎi?
"Is her spouse short or not?"

Nǐmen qù shítáng ma?
"Do you go to the cafeteria?"

Nǐmen qù bu qù shítáng?
"Do you go to the cafeteria or not?"

6. First listen to each comment about **Xiǎo Wáng**, then make a comment about yourself using **bú tài**.

Xiǎo Wáng hěn kùn.
"Little Wang is very sleepy."

Wǒ bú tài kùn.
"I am not too sleepy."

Xiǎo Wáng hěn lèi.
"Little Wang is very tired."

Wǒ bú tài lèi.
"I am not too tired."

Xiǎo Wáng hěn gāo.
"Little Wang is very tall."

Wǒ bú tài gāo.
"I am not too tall."

Xiǎo Wáng zuìjìn hěn hǎo.
"Little Wang has been very well recently."

Wǒ zuìjìn bú tài hǎo.
"I have not been too well recently."

Xiǎo Wáng hěn lǎo.
"Little Wang is very old."

Wǒ bú tài lǎo.
"I am not too old."

Xiǎo Wáng gōngzuò hěn jǐnzhāng.
"Little Wang is very nervous at work."

Wǒ gōngzuò bú tài jǐnzhāng.
"I am not too nervous at work."

7. Transform the following sentences from the **hěn** + STATIVE VERB pattern to the **tǐng...-de** pattern.

Tā hěn kùn.
"He is very sleepy."

Tā tǐng kùnde.
"He is quite sleepy."

Zhōngwén hěn nán.
"Chinese is very hard."

Zhōngwén tǐng nánde.
"Chinese is quite hard."

Wǒ māma hěn máng.
"My mother is very busy."

Wǒ māma tǐng mángde.
"My mother is quite busy."

Nǐ àiren hěn ǎi.
"Your spouse is very short."

Nǐ àiren tǐng ǎide.
"Your spouse is quite short."

Tā bàba hěn lǎo.
"Her father is very old."

Tā bàba tǐng lǎode.
"Her father is quite old."

Nǐ yàngzi hěn jǐnzhāng.
"You look like you're very nervous."

Nǐ yàngzi tǐng jǐnzhāngde.
"You look like you're quite nervous."

Tā zuìjìn gōngzuò hěn lèi.
"He is very tired from work lately."

Tā zuìjìn gōngzuò tǐng lèide.
"He is quite tired from work lately."

Unit 1, Part 4: Transformation and Response Drills

1. Add the surname and title of the wife to the husband's surname and title.

Zhào Xiānsheng "Mr. Zhao"	**Zhào Xiānsheng, Zhào Tàitai** "Mr. and Mrs. Zhao"
Gāo Xiānsheng "Mr. Gao"	**Gāo Xiānsheng, Gāo Tàitai** "Mr. and Mrs. Gao"
Wáng Xiānsheng "Mr. Wang"	**Wáng Xiānsheng, Wáng Tàitai** "Mr. and Mrs. Wang"
Kē Xiānsheng "Mr. Ke"	**Kē Xiānsheng, Kē Tàitai** "Mr. and Mrs. Ke"
Lín Xiānsheng "Mr. Lin"	**Lín Xiānsheng, Lín Tàitai** "Mr. and Mrs. Lin"
Xiè Xiānsheng "Mr. Xie"	**Xiè Xiānsheng, Xiè Tàitai** "Mr. and Mrs. Xie"

2. Add the title **Xiáojie** to each of the following surnames.

Wáng "Wang"	**Wáng Xiáojie** "Miss/Ms. Wang"
Lín "Lin"	**Lín Xiáojie** "Miss/Ms. Lin"
Hé "He"	**Hé Xiáojie** "Miss/Ms. He"
Xiè "Xie"	**Xiè Xiáojie** "Miss/Ms. Xie"
Gāo "Gao"	**Gāo Xiáojie** "Miss/Ms. Gao"
Zhào "Zhao"	**Zhào Xiáojie** "Miss/Ms. Zhao"

3. Add the title **Lǎoshī** to each of the following surnames.

Lín "Lin"	**Lín Lǎoshī** "Teacher Lin"
Xiè "Xie"	**Xiè Lǎoshī** "Teacher Xie"
Gāo "Gao"	**Gāo Lǎoshī** "Teacher Gao"
Zhào "Zhao"	**Zhào Lǎoshī** "Teacher Zhao"

Hé "He"	**Hé Lǎoshī** "Teacher He"
Wáng "Wang"	**Wáng Lǎoshī** "Teacher Wang"

4. Add **qǐng** to the following sentences to create polite imperatives.

Nǐ qù shítáng. "You go to the cafeteria."	**Qǐng nǐ qù shítáng.** "Please go to the cafeteria."
Nǐ qù gōngzuò. "You go work."	**Qǐng nǐ qù gōngzuò.** "Please go work."
Tā huí sùshè. "He goes back to the dormitory."	**Qǐng tā huí sùshè.** "Ask him to please go back to the dormitory."
Nǐmen qù túshūguǎn bàn yìdiǎnr shì. "You go to the library and take care of some stuff."	**Qǐng nǐmen qù túshūguǎn bàn yìdiǎnr shì.** "Please go to the library and take care of some stuff."
Tāmen xiān zǒu. "They leave earlier."	**Qǐng tāmen xiān zǒu.** "Ask them to please leave earlier."

5. Add changed status **le** to the following sentences.

Wǒ děi qù gōngzuò. "I have to go to work."	**Wǒ děi qù gōngzuòle.** "I have to go to work now."
Tā zěmmeyàng? "How is he?"	**Tā zěmmeyàng le?** "What happened to him?"
Tā xiān zǒu. "She leaves earlier."	**Tā xiān zǒule.** "She left earlier already."
Xiǎo Lín qù shítáng. "Little Lin goes to the cafeteria."	**Xiǎo Lín qù shítáng le.** "Little Lin went to the cafeteria."
Shéi bú qù? "Who is not going?"	**Shéi bú qùle?** "Who is not going now?"
Tāmen huí sùshè. "They go back to the dormitory."	**Tāmen huí sùshè le.** "They went back to the dormitory."

6. Add changed status **le** to the following questions ending in **ma**.

Tā māma hǎo ma? "Is her mother well?"	**Tā māma hǎole ma?** "Has her mother gotten well?"
Nǐ jǐnzhāng ma? "Are you nervous?"	**Nǐ jǐnzhāngle ma?** "Have you gotten nervous?"
Wǒmen kéyi huí sùshè ma? "Can we go back to the dormitory?"	**Wǒmen kéyi huí sùshè le ma?** "Can we go back to the dormitory now?"

Tā qù túshūguǎn bàn shì ma?
"Is he going to the library to take care of some stuff?"

Háizi kùn ma?
"Are the kids sleepy?"

Nǐmen qù shítáng ma?
"Are you going to the cafeteria?"

Tā qù túshūguǎn bàn shì le ma?
"Has he gone to the library to take care of some stuff?"

Háizi kùnle ma?
"Have the kids gotten sleepy?"

Nǐmen qù shítáng le ma?
"Have you gone to the cafeteria?"

· ·

Unit 2, Part 1: Transformation and Response Drills

1. Respond to the following questions with an equative verb sentence beginning with **shì**.

Tā shi Měiguo rén ma?
"Is she American?"

Shì, tā shi Měiguo rén.
"Yes, she is American."

Tā shi Zhōngguo rén ma?
"Is he Chinese?"

Shì, tā shi Zhōngguo rén.
"Yes, he is Chinese."

Tā shi Wáng Lǎoshī ma?
"Is she Teacher Wang?"

Shì, tā shi Wáng Lǎoshī.
"Yes, she is Teacher Wang."

Tā shi nǐ àiren ma?
"Is he your spouse?"

Shì, tā shi wǒ àiren.
"Yes, he is my spouse."

Nǐ shi tā bàba ma?
"Are you her father?"

Shì, wǒ shi tā bàba.
"Yes, I am her father."

Nǐ shi tā māma ma?
"Are you his mother?"

Shì, wǒ shi tā māma.
"Yes, I am his mother."

2. Respond to the following questions with a negative equative verb sentence beginning with **bú shi**.

Nǐ shi Zhōngwén lǎoshī ma?
"Are you a Chinese teacher?"

Bú shi, wǒ bú shi Zhōngwén lǎoshī.
"No, I am not a Chinese teacher."

Nǐ shi Lín Xiáojie ma?
"Are you Ms. Lin?"

Bú shi, wǒ bú shi Lín Xiáojie.
"No, I am not Ms. Lin."

Nǐmen shi Jiā'nádà rén ma?
"Are you all Canadian?"

Bú shi, wǒmen bú shi Jiā'nádà rén.
"No, we're not Canadian."

Tā shi Wáng Xiānsheng ma?
"Is he Mr. Wang?"

Bú shi, tā bú shi Wáng Xiānsheng.
"No, he's not Mr. Wang."

3. Respond to the following questions either with an equative verb sentence beginning with **Shì** or with a negative equative verb sentence beginning with **Bú shi**, depending on the cue provided.

Tā shi nǐ bàba ma? (Shì.)
"Is he your dad?" ("Yes.")

Shì, tā shi wǒ bàba.
"Yes, he is my dad."

Tā shi nǐ māma ma? (Bú shi.)
"Is she your mom?" ("No.")

Bú shi, tā bú shi wǒ māma.
"No, she's not my mom."

Qǐng wèn, nǐ shi Bái Lǎoshī ma? (Bú shi.)
"Excuse me, are you Teacher Bai?" ("No.")

Bú shi, wǒ bú shi Bái Lǎoshī.
"No, I'm not Teacher Bai."

Tā shi Huáyì Měiguo rén ma? (Shì.)
"Is he an American of Chinese descent?" ("Yes.")

Shì, tā shi Huáyì Měiguo rén.
"Yes, he's an American of Chinese descent."

Nǐmen shi Táiwān rén ma? (Bú shi.)
"Are you Taiwanese?" ("No.")

Bú shi, wǒmen bú shi Táiwān rén.
"No, we're not Taiwanese."

4. Transform the following statements into questions using **shì bu shi**.

Tā shi Rìběn rén.
"He is Japanese."

Tā shì bu shi Rìběn rén?
"Is he Japanese?"

Nǐ shi tā àiren.
"You are her spouse."

Nǐ shì bu shi tā àiren?
"Are you her spouse?"

Nǐmen shi Xībānyá rén.
"You are Spanish."

Nǐmen shì bu shi Xībānyá rén?
"Are you Spanish?"

Tā shi Wáng Xiáojie.
"She is Miss Wang."

Tā shì bu shi Wáng Xiáojie?
"Is she Miss Wang?"

Nǐ zuìjìn hěn máng.
"You have been very busy recently."

Nǐ zuìjìn shì bu shi hěn máng?
"Have you been very busy lately?"

Tā dào túshūguǎn qù.
"He is going to the library."

Tā shì bu shi dào túshūguǎn qù?
"Is it the case that he's going to the library?"

5. Answer the following questions about nationality using the cues provided.

Tā shi něiguó rén? (Jiā'nádà rén)
"What nationality is he?" ("Canadian")

Tā shi Jiā'nádà rén.
"He's Canadian."

Nǐ àiren shi něiguó rén? (Rìběn rén)
"What nationality is your spouse?" ("Japanese")

Tā shi Rìběn rén.
"She's Japanese."

Nín shi něiguó rén? (Měiguo rén)
"What nationality are you?" ("American")

Wǒ shi Měiguo rén.
"I'm American."

Mǎ Xiáojie shi něiguó rén? (Zhōngguo rén)
"What nationality is Ms. Ma?" ("Chinese")

Mǎ Xiáojie shi Zhōngguo rén.
"Ms. Ma is Chinese."

Xiǎo Lín shi něiguó rén? (Mǎláixīyà rén)
"What nationality is Little Lin?" ("Malaysian")

Xiǎo Lín shi Mǎláixīyà rén.
"Little Lin is Malaysian."

Nǐ lǎoshī shi něiguó rén? (Xīnjiāpō rén)
"What nationality is your teacher?" ("Singaporean")

Wǒ lǎoshī shi Xīnjiāpō rén.
"My teacher is Singaporean."

6. Respond to the following questions about someone's name using the cues provided.

Tā jiào shémme míngzi? (Hé Zhìwén)
"What is his name?"

Tā jiào Hé Zhìwén.
"He is called He Zhiwen."

Nǐ àiren jiào shémme míngzi? (Wáng Dàmíng)
"What is your spouse's name?"

Wǒ àiren jiào Wáng Dàmíng.
"My spouse is called Wang Daming."

Nǐ māma jiào shémme míngzi? (Xiè Wéntíng)
"What is your mom's name?"

Wǒ māma jiào Xiè Wéntíng.
"My mom's name is Xie Wenting."

Nǐ bàba jiào shémme míngzi? (Zhào Guólì)
"What is your dad's name?"

Wǒ bàba jiào Zhào Guólì.
"My dad's name is Zhao Guoli."

Nǐ jiào shémme míngzi? (give your own name)
"What is your name?"

Wǒ jiào...
"My name is..."

7. Negate the following sentences by placing a **bù** before the **dōu**.

Tāmen dōu shi Zhōngguo rén.
"They are all Chinese."

Tāmen bù dōu shi Zhōngguo rén.
"They are not all Chinese."

Tāmen dōu hěn kùn.
"They are all very sleepy."

Tāmen bù dōu hěn kùn.
"They are not all very sleepy."

Wǒmen dōu huí sùshè.
"We are all going back to the dorm."

Wǒmen bù dōu huí sùshè.
"We are not all going back to the dorm."

Wǒmen dōu shi Huáyì Měiguo rén.
"We are all Chinese-Americans."

Wǒmen bù dōu shi Huáyì Měiguo rén.
"We are not all Chinese-Americans."

Nǐmen dōu shi hǎo háizi!
"You are all good children!"

Nǐmen bù dōu shi hǎo háizi!
"You are not all good children!"

Dōu shi xiǎo shì.
"They are all small matters."

Bù dōu shi xiǎo shì.
"They are not all small matters."

8. Disagree with your interlocutor. Answer "It's not THIS person, it's THAT person!" etc.

Shì zhèige rén ma?
"Is it this person?"

Bú shi zhèige rén, shi nèige rén!
"It's not this person, it's that person!"

Shì zhèige háizi ma?
"Was it this kid?"

Bú shi zhèige háizi, shi nèige háizi!
"It wasn't this kid, it was that kid!"

Shì zhèiwèi lǎoshī ma?
"Is it this teacher?"

Bú shi zhèiwèi lǎoshī, shi nèiwèi lǎoshī!
"It isn't this teacher, it's that teacher!"

Shì zhèiwèi tóngxué ma?
"Is it this classmate?"

Bú shi zhèiwèi tóngxué, shi nèiwèi tóngxué!
"It isn't this classmate, it's that classmate!"

Shì zhèige míngzi ma?
"Was it this name?"

Bú shi zhèige míngzi, shi nèige míngzi!
"It wasn't this name, it was that name!"

Shì zhèige sùshè ma?
"Was it this dormitory?"

Bú shi zhèige sùshè, shi nèige sùshè!
"It wasn't this dormitory, it was that dormitory!"

9. Respond to the questions with **něi-** "which?" by using **nèi-** "that."

Shì něige rén?
"Which person was it?"

Shì nèige rén!
"It was that person!"

Shì něige háizi?
"Which child was it?"

Shì nèige háizi!
"It was that child!"

Shì něiwèi lǎoshī?
"Which teacher is it?"

Shì nèiwèi lǎoshī!
"It's that teacher!"

Shì něiwèi tóngxué?
"Which classmate is it?"

Shì nèiwèi tóngxué!
"It's that classmate!"

Shì něige gōngzuò?
"Which job was it?"

Shì nèige gōngzuò!
"It was that job!"

Shì něige shítáng?
"Which dining hall was it?"

Shì nèige shítáng!
"It was that dining hall!"

10. Confirm the truth of what your interlocutor says about the first person by repeating it, but add the new and different information about the other person that is given in the cue by using **kěshi**.

Lǎo Wáng shi Měiguo rén.
(Xiǎo Lín, Mǎláixīyà rén)
"Old Wang is American." ("Little Lin, Malaysian")

Lǎo Wáng shi Měiguo rén, kěshi Xiǎo Lín
shi Mǎláixīyà rén.
"Old Wang is American, but Little Lin is Malaysian."

Lǎo Bái shi Měiguo rén.
(Xiǎo Hé, Xībānyá rén)
"Old Bai is American." ("Little He, Spanish")

Lǎo Bái shi Měiguo rén, kěshi Xiǎo Hé shi
Xībānyá rén.
"Old Bai is American, but Little He is Spanish."

Lǎo Gāo shi Zhōngguo rén.
(Xiǎo Zhào, Rìběn rén)
"Old Gao is Chinese." ("Little Zhao, Japanese")

Lǎo Gāo shi Zhōngguo rén, kěshi Xiǎo Zhào
shi Rìběn rén.
"Old Gao is Chinese, but Little Zhao is Japanese."

Lǎo Lǐ shi Táiwān rén. (Xiǎo Kē, Xīnjiāpō rén)

"Old Li is Taiwanese." ("Little Ke, Singaporean")

Lǎo Lǐ shi Táiwān rén, kěshi Xiǎo Kē shi
Xīnjiāpō rén.
"Old Li is Taiwanese, but Little Ke is Singaporean."

Unit 2, Part 2: Transformation and Response Drills

1. Combine the first noun or pronoun with the noun that follows by adding **-de**.

wǒ, àiren "I, spouse"	**wǒde àiren** "my spouse"
Lǎo Chén, tóngxué "Old Chen, classmate"	**Lǎo Chénde tóngxué** "Old Chen's classmate"
tā, bàba "he/she, father"	**tāde bàba** "his/her father"
nǐmen, sùshè "you all, dormitory"	**nǐmende sùshè** "your dormitory"
tāmen, māma "they, mother"	**tāmende māma** "their mother"
Zhào tóngxué, tóngwū "classmate Zhao, roommate"	**Zhào tóngxuéde tóngwū** "classmate Zhao's roommate"

2. Transform the sentences with **lái** or **qù** followed directly by a place word to the **dào...lái** or **dào...qù** pattern.

Hěn gāoxìng nǐ lái Běijīng! "I'm glad you've come to Beijing!"	**Hěn gāoxìng nǐ dào Běijīng lái!** "I'm glad you've come to Beijing!"
Huānyíng nǐ lái Táiwān! "Welcome to Taiwan!"	**Huānyíng nǐ dào Táiwān lái!** "Welcome to Taiwan!"
Qǐng nǐ qù wǒde sùshè. "Please go to my dormitory."	**Qǐng nǐ dào wǒde sùshè qù.** "Please go to my dormitory."
Búyào qù túshūguǎn! "Don't go to the library!"	**Búyào dào túshūguǎn qù!** "Don't go to the library!"
Tā qù Rìběn le. "He went to Japan."	**Tā dào Rìběn qùle.** "He went to Japan."
Nǐ yīnggāi lái wǒde gōngsī. "You should come to my company."	**Nǐ yīnggāi dào wǒde gōngsī lái.** "You should come to my company."

3. Change the following imperative sentences to negative imperatives by using **bié**.

Qǐng nǐ qù gōngzuò. "Please go to work."	**Qǐng nǐ bié qù gōngzuò.** "Please don't go to work."
Qǐng tāmen lái Táiwān. "Ask them to come to Taiwan."	**Qǐng tāmen bié lái Táiwān.** "Ask them not to come to Taiwan."
Chén Xiáojie, qǐng zuò. "Miss Chen, please sit."	**Chén Xiáojie, qǐng bié zuò.** "Miss Chen, please don't sit."

Bàba, qǐng zǒu.
"Father, please go."

Bàba, qǐng bié zǒu.
"Father, please don't go."

Qǐng nǐmen jiào wǒ Lǎo Chén.
"You all please call me Old Chen."

Qǐng nǐmen bié jiào wǒ Lǎo Chén.
"You all please don't call me Old Chen."

4. Change the following negative imperative sentences with **búyào** to positive imperatives by deleting the **búyào**.

Qǐng nǐ búyào qù túshūguǎn.
"Please don't go to the library."

Qǐng nǐ qù túshūguǎn.
"Please go to the library."

Qǐng nǐ búyào huí sùshè.
"Please don't go back to the dormitory."

Qǐng nǐ huí sùshè.
"Please go back to the dormitory."

Qǐng tāmen búyào lái Měiguo.
"Ask them not to come to the States."

Qǐng tāmen lái Měiguo.
"Ask them to come to the States."

Qǐng nǐmen búyào qù Zhōngguo.
"Please don't go to China."

Qǐng nǐmen qù Zhōngguo.
"Please go to China."

Qǐng nǐ búyào zèmme chēnghu wǒ.
"Please don't address me in this way."

Qǐng nǐ zèmme chēnghu wǒ.
"Please address me in this way."

Qǐng nǐmen búyào qù gōngzuò.
"Please don't go to work."

Qǐng nǐmen qù gōngzuò.
"Please go to work."

5. Respond to each question using the cue provided.

Zhè shi shéide lǎoshī? (wǒde)
"This is whose teacher?" ("my")

Zhè shi wǒde lǎoshī.
"This is my teacher."

Zhè shi shéide háizi? (nǐde)
"Whose kid is this?" ("your")

Zhè shi nǐde háizi.
"This is your kid."

Zhè shi shéide bàba? (tāmende)
"Whose father is this?" ("their")

Zhè shi tāmende bàba.
"This is their father."

Nà shi shéide àiren? (wǒde)
"Whose spouse is that?" ("my")

Nà shi wǒde àiren.
"That is my spouse."

Nà shi shéide māma? (tāmende)
"Whose mother is that?" ("their")

Nà shi tāmende māma.
"That is their mother."

Zhè shi shéide tóngxué? (nǐmende)
"Whose classmate is this?" ("your")

Zhè shi nǐmende tóngxué.
"This is your classmate."

Unit 2, Part 3: Transformation and Response Drills

1. Transform the polite questions with **guìxìng** to more ordinary questions with **xìng shémme**. Remember also to change polite **nín** to ordinary **nǐ**.

Nín guìxìng?
"What's your last name?"

Nín guìxìng?
"What's your last name?"

Nǐ xìng shémme?
"What's your last name?"

Nèiwèi nǚshì guìxìng?
"What's that lady's last name?"

Nèiwèi nǚshì xìng shémme?
"What's that lady's last name?"

Nèiwèi lǎoshī guìxìng?
"What's that teacher's last name?"

Nèiwèi lǎoshī xìng shémme?
"What's that teacher's last name?"

Qǐng wèn, xiáojie, nín guìxìng?
"Excuse me, Miss, what's your last name?"

Qǐng wèn, xiáojie, nǐ xìng shémme?
"Excuse me, Miss, what's your last name?"

Zhèiwèi dàxué xiàozhǎng guìxìng?
"What's this college president's last name?"

Zhèiwèi dàxué xiàozhǎng xìng shémme?
"What's this college president's last name?"

2. Explain that, by golly, your roommate, classmate, colleague, etc. has the same surname as the speaker's!

Wǒde tóngwū xìng Gāo.
"My roommate's last name is Gao."

Wǒde tóngwū yě xìng Gāo!
"My roommate's last name is also Gao!"

Wǒde tóngxué xìng Lín.
"My classmate's last name is Lin."

Wǒde tóngxué yě xìng Lín!
"My classmate's last name is also Lin!"

Wǒde tóngshì xìng Chén.
"My colleague's last name is Chen."

Wǒde tóngshì yě xìng Chén!
"My colleague's last name is also Chen!"

Wǒde Zhōngwén lǎoshī xìng Wú.
"My Chinese teacher's last name is Wu."

Wǒde Zhōngwén lǎoshī yě xìng Wú!
"My Chinese teacher's last name is also Wu!"

Wǒ māma xìng Mǎ.
"My mom's last name is Ma."

Wǒ māma yě xìng Mǎ!
"My mom's last name is also Ma!"

Wǒmende xiàozhǎng xìng Hé.
"Our college president's surname is He."

Wǒmende xiàozhǎng yě xìng Hé!
"Our college president's surname is also He!"

3. Add **ba** to the following sentences to indicate that you think what you said is probably so.

Nǐ yě shi lǎoshī.
"You are a teacher, too."

Nǐ yě shi lǎoshī ba?
"You are a teacher too, I guess?"

Tā shi nǐde tóngshì.
"She is your co-worker."

Tā shi nǐde tóngshì ba?
"She is your co-worker, I suppose?"

Xiǎo Zhào bú shi Zhōngguo rén.
"Little Zhao is not Chinese."

Xiǎo Zhào bú shi Zhōngguo rén ba?
"I suppose Little Zhao is not Chinese?"

Nǐ zài Wàijiāobù gōngzuò.
"You work at the Foreign Ministry."

Nǐ zài Wàijiāobù gōngzuò ba?
"I guess you work at the Foreign Ministry?"

Chén Xiáojie shi Mǎláixīyà rén.
"Miss Chen is Malaysian."

Chén Xiáojie shi Mǎláixīyà rén ba?
"Miss Chen is Malaysian, I guess?"

Tāmen bú rènshi nǐ.
"They are not acquainted with you."

Tāmen bú rènshi nǐ ba?
"They are not acquainted with you, I assume?"

4. Respond to the following questions using the cue provided.

Nǐ zài nǎr gōngzuò a? (shítáng)
"Where do you work?" ("cafeteria")

Wǒ zài shítáng gōngzuò.
"I work at the cafeteria."

Nǐmen zài nǎr gōngzuò a? (dàshǐguǎn)
"Where do you all work?" ("embassy")

Wǒmen zài dàshǐguǎn gōngzuò.
"We work at the embassy."

Tā zài nǎr gōngzuò a? (dàxué)
"Where does she work?" ("university")

Tā zài dàxué gōngzuò.
"She works at the university."

Tāmen zài nǎr gōngzuò a? (túshūguǎn)
"Where do they work?" ("library")

Tāmen zài túshūguǎn gōngzuò.
"They work at the library."

Xiǎo Chén zài nǎr gōngzuò a? (gōngsī)
"Where does Little Chen work?" ("company")

Xiǎo Chén zài gōngsī gōngzuò.
"Little Chen works at the company."

Lǎo Zhào zài nǎr gōngzuò a? (Wàijiāobù)
"Where does Old Zhao work?" ("Foreign Ministry")

Lǎo Zhào zài Wàijiāobù gōngzuò.
"Old Zhao works at the Foreign Ministry."

Unit 2, Part 4: Transformation and Response Drills

1. Transform the following sentences from **bù** to past negative with **méi.**

Wǒ bù lái.
"I'm not coming."

Wǒ méi lái.
"I didn't come."

Wǒ bù zǒu.
"I'm not leaving."

Wǒ méi zǒu.
"I didn't leave."

Wǒ bú dài míngpiàn.
"I don't carry name cards."

Wǒ méi dài míngpiàn.
"I didn't carry name cards."

Tā bú qù Zhōngguo.
"She's not going to China."

Tā méi qù Zhōngguo.
"She didn't go to China."

Nǐ yě bú wèn zěmme qù.
"And you don't ask how to go."

Nǐ yě méi wèn zěmme qù.
"And you didn't ask how to go."

Nǐmen bù huí sùshè ma?
"You're not going back to the dorm?"

Nǐmen méi huí sùshè ma?
"You didn't go back to the dorm?"

Nǐmen bú qù gōngsī ma?
"You're not going to the company?"

Nǐmen méi qù gōngsī ma?
"You didn't go to the company?"

2. Transform the following sentences with the coverb **zài** describing where someone works to noun phrases with **-de** that indicate a person's affiliation.

Nèiwèi Shī Xiáojie zài Zhōng-Měi Màoyì Gōngsī gōngzuò.
"That Miss Shi works at the Sino-American Trading Company."

Zhōng-Měi Màoyì Gōngsīde nèiwèi Shī Xiáojie
"that Miss Shi from Sino-American trading company"

Nèiwèi Mǎ Xiáojie zài Měiguo Dàshǐguǎn gōngzuò.
"That Ms. Ma works at the American Embassy."

Měiguo Dàshǐguǎnde nèiwèi Mǎ Xiáojie
"that Ms. Ma from the American Embassy"

Nèiwèi Hé Lǎoshī zài Táiwān Dàxué gōngzuò.
"That Prof. He works at Taiwan University."

Táiwān Dàxuéde nèiwèi Hé Lǎoshī
"that Prof. He from Taiwan University"

Nèiwèi Wú Xiáojie zài Wàijiāobù gōngzuò.
"That Miss Wu works at the Foreign Ministry."

Wàijiāobùde nèiwèi Wú Xiáojie
"that Miss Wu from the Foreign Ministry"

3. Transform the sentences with **bù dōu** to **dōu bù.**

Tāmen bù dōu shi Rìběn rén.
"They are not all Japanese."

Tāmen dōu bú shi Rìběn rén.
"They all are not Japanese."

Wǒmen bù dōu zài Wàijiāobù gōngzuò.
"We don't all work at the Foreign Ministry."

Wǒmen dōu bú zài Wàijiāobù gōngzuò.
"We all don't work at the Foreign Ministry."

Tāmen bù dōu rènshì Wáng Xiáojie.
"They don't all know Ms. Wang."

Tāmen dōu bú rènshì Wáng Xiáojie.
"None of them knows Ms. Wang."

Wǒmen bù dōu xuéxí Zhōngwén.
"We don't all learn Chinese."

Wǒmen dōu bù xuéxí Zhōngwén.
"None of us is learning Chinese."

Tāmen bù dōu huānyíng wǒ dào Běijīng qù.
"Not all of them welcome me to go to Beijing."

Tāmen dōu bù huānyíng wǒ dào Běijīng qù.
"None of them welcomes me to go to Beijing."

4. Transform the expressions with **zhèi-** to **nèi-** and also add **yě**.

Zhèiwèi xiānsheng xìng Wáng.
"This gentleman's last name is Wang."

Nèiwèi xiānsheng yě xìng Wáng.
"That gentleman's last name is also Wang."

Zhèiwèi tàitai xìng Bái.
"This lady's last name is Bai."

Nèiwèi tàitai yě xìng Bái.
"That lady's last name is also Bai."

Zhèiwèi xiáojie xìng Lín.
"This young lady's last name is Lin."

Nèiwèi xiáojie yě xìng Lín.
"That young lady's last name is also Lin."

Zhèige háizi hěn lèi.
"This child is very tired."

Nèige háizi yě hěn lèi.
"That child is also very tired."

Zhèiwèi jīnglǐ hěn gāoxìng.
"This manager is very happy."

Nèiwèi jīnglǐ yě hěn gāoxìng.
"That manager is also very happy."

Zhèige Měiguo rén wǒ bú rènshì.
"I don't know this American."

Nèige Měiguo rén wǒ yě bú rènshì.
"I don't know that American either."

Zhèige dàxué hěn xīn.
"This university is very new."

Nèige dàxué yě hěn xīn.
"That university is also very new."

5. Use **gēn** to join the second noun or pronoun to the first noun or pronoun.

wǒ (nǐ)
"I" ("you")

wǒ gēn nǐ
"I and you"

wǒ (tā)
"I" ("he")

wǒ gēn tā
"I and he"

wǒmen (nǐmen)
"we" ("you")

wǒmen gēn nǐmen
"we and you"

wǒmen (tāmen)
"we" ("they")

wǒmen gēn tāmen
"we and they"

Lǎo Lǐ (Xiǎo Bái)
"Old Li" ("Little Bai")

Lǎo Lǐ gēn Xiǎo Bái
"Old Li and Little Bai"

àiren (háizi)
"spouse" ("child")

àiren gēn háizi
"spouse and child"

xiānsheng (tàitai)
"husband" ("wife")

xiānsheng gēn tàitai
"husband and wife"

Zhōngguo (Táiwān)
"Mainland China" ("Taiwan")

Zhōngguo gēn Táiwān
"Mainland China and Taiwan"

Zhōngguo rén (Měiguo rén)
"Chinese" ("Americans")

Zhōngguo rén gēn Měiguo rén
"Chinese and Americans"

6. Transform each phrase or sentence that you hear into a politer equivalent.

Nǐ hǎo!
"How are you?"

Nín hǎo!
"How do you do?"

Nǐ xìng shémme?
"What's your last name?"

Nín guìxìng?
"What is your honorable surname?"

zhèige xiānsheng
"this man"

zhèiwèi xiānsheng
"this gentleman"

nèige tàitai
"that lady"

nèiwèi tàitai
"that lady"

Něige xiáojie?
"Which young woman?"

Něiwèi xiáojie?
"Which young lady?"

zhèige xiàozhǎng
"this school principal"

zhèiwèi xiàozhǎng
"this school principal"

nèige zǒngjīnglǐ
"that general manager"

nèiwèi zǒngjīnglǐ
"that general manager"

Něige nǚshì?
"Which lady?"

Něiwèi nǚshì?
"Which lady?"

yíge lǎoshī
"a teacher"

yíwèi lǎoshī
"a teacher"

Unit 3, Part 1: Transformation and Response Drills

1. Say the number that comes after the number you hear.

liù "six"	**qī** "seven"
jiǔ "nine"	**shí** "ten"
yī "one"	**èr** "two"
sì "four"	**wǔ** "five"
qī "seven"	**bā** "eight"
èr "two"	**sān** "three"
bā "eight"	**jiǔ** "nine"
sān "three"	**sì** "four"
wǔ "five"	**liù** "six"

2. Say the number that comes before the number you hear.

qī "seven"	**liù** "six"
shí "ten"	**jiǔ** "nine"
èr "two"	**yī** "one"
jiǔ "nine"	**bā** "eight"
wǔ "five"	**sì** "four"
sān "three"	**èr** "two"
liù "six"	**wǔ** "five"

bā
"eight"

qī
"seven"

sì
"four"

sān
"three"

3. Comment that, in each case, you have one more student in your class than the speaker does.

Wǒmen bānshang yǒu jiǔge tóngxué.
"Our class has nine classmates."

Wǒmen bānshang yǒu shíge tóngxué.
"Our class has ten classmates."

Wǒmen bānshang yǒu liǎngge tóngxué.
"Our class has two classmates."

Wǒmen bānshang yǒu sān'ge tóngxué.
"Our class has three classmates."

Wǒmen bānshang yǒu liùge tóngxué.
"Our class has six classmates."

Wǒmen bānshang yǒu qíge tóngxué.
"Our class has seven classmates."

Wǒmen bānshang yǒu sìge tóngxué.
"Our class has four classmates."

Wǒmen bānshang yǒu wǔge tóngxué.
"Our class has five classmates."

Wǒmen bānshang yǒu sān'ge tóngxué.
"Our class has three classmates."

Wǒmen bānshang yǒu sìge tóngxué.
"Our class has four classmates."

Wǒmen bānshang yǒu qíge tóngxué.
"Our class has seven classmates."

Wǒmen bānshang yǒu báge tóngxué.
"Our class has eight classmates."

Wǒmen bānshang yǒu wǔge tóngxué.
"Our class has five classmates."

Wǒmen bānshang yǒu liùge tóngxué.
"Our class has six classmates."

Wǒmen bānshang yǒu báge tóngxué.
"Our class has eight classmates."

Wǒmen bānshang yǒu jiǔge tóngxué.
"Our class has nine classmates."

4. Comment that, in each case, the ratio of male students to female students in your class is the exact reverse of the speaker's class.

Wǒmen bānshang yǒu liǎngge nánshēng, yíge nǚshēng.
"Our class has two guys, one girl."

Wǒmen bānshang yǒu yíge nánshēng, liǎngge nǚshēng.
"Our class has one guy, two girls."

Wǒmen bānshang yǒu sān'ge nánshēng, sìge nǚshēng.
"Our class has three guys, four girls."

Wǒmen bānshang yǒu sìge nánshēng, sān'ge nǚshēng.
"Our class has four guys, three girls."

Wǒmen bānshang yǒu wǔge nánshēng, liùge nǚshēng.
"Our class has five guys, six girls."

Wǒmen bānshang yǒu liùge nánshēng, wǔge nǚshēng.
"Our class has six guys, five girls."

Wǒmen bānshang yǒu qíge nánshēng, báge nǚshēng.
"Our class has seven guys, eight girls."

Wǒmen bānshang yǒu báge nánshēng, qíge nǚshēng.
"Our class has eight guys, seven girls."

Wǒmen bānshang yǒu jiǔge nánshēng, shíge nǚshēng.
"Our class has nine guys, ten girls."

Wǒmen bānshang yǒu shíge nánshēng, jiǔge nǚshēng.
"Our class has ten guys, nine girls."

5. Use the conjunction **nà** and the final particle **ne** to introduce the new topic indicated.

Tāmen bānshang yǒu shíge tóngxué.
(nǐmen bānshang)
"Their class has ten classmates." ("your class")

Nà, nǐmen bānshang ne?

"And how about your class?"

Tā yǒu sānwèi Zhōngwén lǎoshī. (nǐ)
"He has three Chinese teachers." ("you")

Nà, nǐ ne?
"And what about you?"

Wǒmende gōngsī yǒu liǎngwèi jīnglǐ. (nǐde gōngsī)
"Our company has two managers." ("your company")

Nà, nǐde gōngsī ne?
"And what about your company?"

Tāde lǎoshī dōu shi nánde. (nǐde lǎoshī)
"Her teachers are all male." ("your teachers")

Nà, nǐde lǎoshī ne?
"And what about your teachers?"

Tā xìng Chén. (nǐ)
"Her last name is Chen." ("you")

Nà, nǐ ne?
"And what about you?"

6. Convert the following Beijing-style pronunciations to non-Beijing-style pronunciations.

yìdiǎnr
"a little bit"

yìdiǎn
"a little bit"

shìr
"matter"

shì
"matter"

yíxiàr
"(softens the verb)"

yíxià
"(softens the verb)"

tóngwūr
"roommate"

tóngwū
"roommate"

yíbànr
"half"

yíbàn
"half"

yíbànr yíbànr
"half and half"

yíbàn yíbàn
"half and half"

Unit 3, Part 2: Transformation and Response Drills

1. In answering the question, comment that you are, in each case, three years older than your interlocutor.

Wǒ jīnnián shíliùsuì. Nǐ ne?
"I am sixteen this year. And you?"

Wǒ jīnnián shíjiǔsuì.
"I am nineteen this year."

Wǒ jīnnián èrshiyīsuì. Nǐ ne?
"I am twenty-one this year. And you?"

Wǒ jīnnián èrshisìsuì.
"I am twenty-four this year."

Wǒ jīnnián sānshibāsuì. Nǐ ne?
"I am thirty-eight this year. And you?"

Wǒ jīnnián sìshiyīsuì.
"I am forty-one this year."

Wǒ jīnnián sìshiwǔsuì. Nǐ ne?
"I am forty-five this year. And you?"

Wǒ jīnnián sìshibāsuì.
"I am forty-eight this year."

Wǒ jīnnián wǔshiqīsuì. Nǐ ne?
"I am fifty-seven this year. And you?"

Wǒ jīnnián liùshisuì.
"I am sixty this year."

Wǒ jīnnián liùshiliùsuì. Nǐ ne?
"I am sixty-six this year. And you?"

Wǒ jīnnián liùshijiǔsuì.
"I am sixty-nine this year."

2. In responding, comment that your mother is, in each case, six years younger than your interlocutor's mother.

Wǒ mǔqīn jīnnián sìshibāsuì le. Nǐ mǔqīn ne?
"My mother is 48 this year. And your mother?"

Wǒ mǔqīn jīnnián sìshi'èrsuì le.
"My mother is 42 this year."

Wǒ mǔqīn jīnnián sānshiliùsuì le. Nǐ mǔqīn ne?
"My mother is 36 this year. And your mother?"

Wǒ mǔqīn jīnnián sānshisuì le.
"My mother is 30 this year."

Wǒ mǔqīn jīnnián wǔshiqīsuì le. Nǐ mǔqīn ne?
"My mother is 57 this year. And your mother?"

Wǒ mǔqīn jīnnián wǔshiyīsuì le.
"My mother is 51 this year."

Wǒ mǔqīn jīnnián bāshiliùsuì le. Nǐ mǔqīn ne?
"My mother is 86 this year. And your mother?"

Wǒ mǔqīn jīnnián bāshisuì le.
"My mother is 80 this year."

Wǒ mǔqīn jīnnián qīshiwǔsuì le. Nǐ mǔqīn ne?
"My mother is 75 this year. And your mother?"

Wǒ mǔqīn jīnnián liùshijiǔsuì le.
"My mother is 69 this year."

Wǒ mǔqīn jīnnián liùshisānsuì le. Nǐ mǔqīn ne?
"My mother is 63 this year. And your mother?"

Wǒ mǔqīn jīnnián wǔshiqīsuì le.
"My mother is 57 this year."

3. Reduplicate each single-syllable verb and add **kàn**.

Nǐ zuò.
"You sit."

Nǐ zuòzuo kàn.
"Try and sit on it."

Nǐ shuō.
"You say."

Nǐ shuōshuo kàn.
"Try and say it."

Nǐ tīng.
"You listen."

Nǐ tīngting kàn.
"Try and listen to it."

Nǐ xiǎng.
"You think."

Nǐ xiǎngxiang kàn.
"Try and think of it/something."

Nǐ wèn.
"You ask."

Nǐ wènwen kàn.
"Try and ask."

Nǐ cāi.
"You guess."

Nǐ cāicai kàn.
"Try and guess."

4. Replace the final **ba** that indicates supposition with the tag question **duì bu dui**.

Zhè shi nǐ mèimei ba?
"This is your sister, I suppose?"

Zhè shi nǐ mèimei, duì bu dui?
"This is your sister, right?"

Tā hěn ài tā xiānsheng ba?
"She loves her husband, I suppose?"

Tā hěn ài tā xiānsheng, duì bu dui?
"She loves her husband, right?"

Nǐmen dōu shi Rìběn rén ba?
"You are all Japanese, I suppose?"

Nǐmen dōu shi Rìběn rén, duì bu dui?
"You are all Japanese, right?"

Tāmende fùqin wǔshisuì le ba?
"Their father is fifty, I suppose?"

Tāmende fùqin wǔshisuì le, duì bu dui?
"Their father is fifty, right?"

Nèiwèi xiáojie shi Lín Xiáojie ba?
"That young lady is Ms. Lin, I suppose?"

Nèiwèi xiáojie shi Lín Xiáojie, duì bu dui?
"That young lady is Ms. Lin, right?"

Zhèiwèi shi nǐ gēge ba?
"This is your brother, I suppose?"

Zhèiwèi shi nǐ gēge, duì bu dui?
"This is your brother, right?"

5. Replace the final **ba** that indicates supposition with the tag question **shì bu shi**.

Tā shi nǐ fùqin ba?
"He's your father, I suppose?"

Tā shi nǐ fùqin, shì bu shi?
"He's your father, isn't he?"

Wǒmen hěn kě'ài ba?
"We're very cute, I suppose?"

Wǒmen hěn kě'ài, shì bu shi?
"We're very cute, aren't we?"

Wáng Jīnglǐ sìshisuì le ba?
"Manager Wang is forty years old, I suppose?"

Wáng Jīnglǐ sìshisuì le, shì bu shi?
"Manager Wang is forty years old, isn't he?"

Tā xiǎng qù Zhōngguo ba?
"He wants to go to China, I suppose?"

Tā xiǎng qù Zhōngguo, shì bu shi?
"He wants to go to China, doesn't he?"

Nǐmen lèile ba?
"You're tired, I suppose?"

Nǐmen lèile, shì bu shi?
"You're tired, aren't you?"

Unit 3, Part 3: Transformation and Response Drills

1. Answer each **něige** question with **nèige**.

Něige shítáng?
"Which cafeteria?"

Nèige shítáng!
"That cafeteria!"

Něige túshūguǎn?
"Which library?"

Nèige túshūguǎn!
"That library!"

Něige dàshǐguǎn?
"Which embassy?"

Nèige dàshǐguǎn!
"That embassy!"

Něige gōngshìbāo?
"Which briefcase?"

Nèige gōngshìbāo!
"That briefcase!"

Něige dàizi?
"Which bag?"

Nèige dàizi!
"That bag!"

Něige bēizi?
"Which cup?"

Nèige bēizi!
"That cup!"

2. Now answer each **něige** question with **zhèige**.

Něige dānwèi?
"Which unit?"

Zhèige dānwèi.
"This unit."

Něige míngzi?
"Which name?"

Zhèige míngzi.
"This name."

Něige bēibāo?
"Which backpack?"

Zhèige bēibāo.
"This backpack."

Něige dàxué?
"Which college?"

Zhèige dàxué.
"This college."

Něige sùshè?
"Which dormitory?"

Zhèige sùshè.
"This dormitory."

Něige bān?
"Which class?"

Zhèige bān.
"This class."

3. Add **le** after each instance of **tài** + STATIVE VERB.

tài guì
"too expensive"

Tài guìle.
"It's too expensive."

tài piányi
"too cheap"

Tài piányile.
"It's too cheap."

tài kě'ài
"too cute"

Tài kě'àile.
"It's too cute."

tài gāoxìng
"too happy"

Tài gāoxìngle.
"She's too happy."

tài xiǎo
"too small"

Tài xiǎole.
"It's too small."

tài lèi
"too tired"

Tài lèile.
"I'm too tired."

tài nán
"too hard"

Tài nánle.
"It was too hard."

tài yǒu yìsi
"too interesting"

Tài yǒu yìsi le.
"It's too interesting."

tài méi yìsi
"too uninteresting"

Tài méi yìsi le.
"It's too uninteresting."

4. Reduplicate the following single-syllable verbs.

kàn
"look"

kànkan
"take a look"

shuō
"say"

shuōshuo
"say something"

tīng
"listen"

tīngting
"listen"

zuò
"sit"

zuòzuo
"take a seat"

cāi
"guess"

cāicai
"take a guess"

wèn
"ask"

wènwen
"ask"

5. Add **ba** to the following sentences to create suggestions.

Nǐ qù.
"You go."

Nǐ qù ba.
"Why don't you go."

Nǐ mǎi liǎngge.
"You buy two."

Nǐ mǎi liǎngge ba.
"Why don't you buy two?"

Wǒmen zǒu.
"We go."

Wǒmen zǒu ba.
"Let's go."

Nǐmen huí sùshè.
"You go back to the dormitory."

Nǐmen huí sùshè ba.
"Why don't you go back to the dormitory."

Xiǎo Wáng, nǐ bēizi gěi wǒ.
"Little Wang, give me your cup."

Xiǎo Wáng, nǐ bēizi gěi wǒ ba.
"Little Wang, why don't you give me your cup."

Wǒmen qù shítáng.
"We go to the cafeteria."

Wǒmen qù shítáng ba.
"Let's go to the cafeteria."

6. In each case, answer in the negative and state that you have 100 items more than the speaker thinks.

Nǐ yǒu yībǎige ma?
"Do you have a hundred?"

Bú shi, wǒ yǒu liǎngbǎige.
"No, I have two hundred."

Nǐ yǒu liǎngbǎige ma?
"Do you have two hundred?"

Bú shi, wǒ yǒu sānbǎige.
"No, I have three hundred."

Nǐ yǒu sānbǎige ma?
"Do you have three hundred?"

Bú shi, wǒ yǒu sìbǎige.
"No, I have four hundred."

Nǐ yǒu sìbǎige ma?
"Do you have four hundred?"

Bú shi, wǒ yǒu wǔbǎige.
"No, I have five hundred."

Nǐ yǒu wǔbǎige ma?
"Do you have five hundred?"

Bú shi, wǒ yǒu liùbǎige.
"No, I have six hundred."

Nǐ yǒu liùbǎige ma?
"Do you have six hundred?"

Bú shi, wǒ yǒu qībǎige.
"No, I have seven hundred."

Nǐ yǒu qībǎige ma?
"Do you have seven hundred?"

Bú shi, wǒ yǒu bābǎige.
"No, I have eight hundred."

Nǐ yǒu bābǎige ma?
"Do you have eight hundred?"

Bú shi, wǒ yǒu jiǔbǎige.
"No, I have nine hundred."

7. In each case, using **zhǐ**, answer in the negative and state that you have $1000 less than the speaker thinks.

Nǐ yǒu jiǔqiānkuài ma?
"Do you have nine thousand dollars?"

Bú shi, wǒ zhǐ yǒu bāqiānkuài.
"No, I only have eight thousand dollars."

Nǐ yǒu bāqiānkuài ma?
"Do you have eight thousand dollars?"

Bú shi, wǒ zhǐ yǒu qīqiānkuài.
"No, I only have seven thousand dollars."

Nǐ yǒu qīqiānkuài ma?
"Do you have seven thousand dollars?"

Bú shi, wǒ zhǐ yǒu liùqiānkuài.
"No, I only have six thousand dollars."

Nǐ yǒu liùqiānkuài ma?
"Do you have six thousand dollars?"

Bú shi, wǒ zhǐ yǒu wǔqiānkuài.
"No, I only have five thousand dollars."

Nǐ yǒu wǔqiānkuài ma?
"Do you have five thousand dollars?"

Bú shi, wǒ zhǐ yǒu sìqiānkuài.
"No, I only have four thousand dollars."

Nǐ yǒu sìqiānkuài ma?
"Do you have four thousand dollars?"

Bú shi, wǒ zhǐ yǒu sānqiānkuài.
"No, I only have three thousand dollars."

Nǐ yǒu sānqiānkuài ma?
"Do you have three thousand dollars?"

Bú shi, wǒ zhǐ yǒu liǎngqiānkuài.
"No, I only have two thousand dollars."

Nǐ yǒu liǎngqiānkuài ma?
"Do you have two thousand dollars?"

Bú shi, wǒ zhǐ yǒu yìqiānkuài.
"No, I only have one thousand dollars."

8. You will be asked if you and your colleagues at a second hand store buy a certain type of item. Explain that you don't buy this type of item, but you do sell them.

Nǐmen mǎi bēizi ma?
"Do you buy cups?"

Wǒmen bù mǎi bēizi, kěshi wǒmen mài bēizi.
"We don't buy cups, but we do sell cups."

Nǐmen mǎi bēibāo ma?
"Do you buy backpacks?"

Wǒmen bù mǎi bēibāo, kěshi wǒmen mài bēibāo.
"We don't buy backpacks, but we do sell backpacks."

Nǐmen mǎi gōngshìbāo ma?
"Do you buy briefcases?"

Wǒmen bù mǎi gōngshìbāo, kěshi wǒmen mài gōngshìbāo.
"We don't buy briefcases, but we do sell briefcases."

Nǐmen mǎi dàizi ma?
"Do you buy bags?"

Wǒmen bù mǎi dàizi, kěshi wǒmen mài dàizi.
"We don't buy bags, but we do sell bags."

Nǐmen mǎi míngpiàn ma?
"Do you buy name cards?"

Wǒmen bù mǎi míngpiàn, kěshi wǒmen mài míngpiàn.
"We don't buy name cards, but we do sell name cards."

9. Add or subtract as requested.

Yī jiā yī shi duōshǎo?
"1 + 1 is how much?"

Yī jiā yī shi èr.
"1 + 1 is 2."

Èr jiǎn yī shi duōshǎo?
"2 − 1 is how much?"

Èr jiǎn yī shi yī.
"2 − 1 is 1."

Qīshí jiā shí shi duōshǎo?
"70 + 10 is how much?"

Qīshí jiā shí shi bāshí.
"70 + 10 is 80."

Liùshí jiǎn shí shi duōshǎo?
"60 − 10 is how much?"

Liùshí jiǎn shí shi wǔshí.
"60 − 10 is 50."

Sìshisān jiā wǔshiwǔ shi duōshǎo?
"43 + 55 is how much?"

Sìshisān jiā wǔshiwǔ shi jiǔshibā.
"43 + 55 is 98."

Sānshiqī jiǎn shí'èr shi duōshǎo?
"37 − 12 is how much?"

Sānshiqī jiǎn shí'èr shi èrshiwǔ.
"37 − 12 is 25."

Sìqiān jiā liǎngqiān shi duōshǎo?
"4,000 + 2,000 is how much?"

Sìqiān jiā liǎngqiān shi liùqiān.
"4,000 + 2,000 is 6,000."

Jiǔbǎi jiǔshijiǔ jiǎn yībǎi shi duōshǎo?
"999 − 100 is how much?"

Jiǔbǎi jiǔshijiǔ jiǎn yībǎi shi bābǎi jiǔshijiǔ.
"999 − 100 is 899."

· ·

Unit 3, Part 4: Transformation and Response Drills

1. In each case, indicate that the time is already one hour later than your interlocutor thinks.

Xiànzài yīdiǎn zhōng ba?
"It's now one o'clock, right?"

Bú shi, yǐjīng liǎngdiǎn le.
"No, it's already two."

Xiànzài liǎngdiǎn zhōng ba?
"It's now two o'clock, right?"

Bú shi, yǐjīng sāndiǎn le.
"No, it's already three."

Xiànzài sāndiǎn zhōng ba?
"It's now three o'clock, right?"

Bú shi, yǐjīng sìdiǎn le.
"No, it's already four."

Xiànzài sìdiǎn zhōng ba?
"It's now four o'clock, right?"

Bú shi, yǐjīng wǔdiǎn le.
"No, it's already five."

Xiànzài wǔdiǎn zhōng ba?
"It's now five o'clock, right?"

Bú shi, yǐjīng liùdiǎn le.
"No, it's already six."

Xiànzài liùdiǎn zhōng ba?
"It's now six o'clock, right?"

Bú shi, yǐjīng qīdiǎn le.
"No, it's already seven."

Xiànzài qīdiǎn zhōng ba?
"It's now seven o'clock, right?"

Bú shi, yǐjīng bādiǎn le.
"No, it's already eight."

Xiànzài bādiǎn zhōng ba?
"It's now eight o'clock, right?"

Bú shi, yǐjīng jiǔdiǎn le.
"No, it's already nine."

Xiànzài jiǔdiǎn zhōng ba?
"It's now nine o'clock, right?"

Bú shi, yǐjīng shídiǎn le.
"No, it's already ten."

Xiànzài shídiǎn zhōng ba?
"It's now ten o'clock, right?"

Bú shi, yǐjīng shíyīdiǎn le.
"No, it's already eleven."

Xiànzài shíyīdiǎn zhōng ba?
"It's now eleven o'clock, right?"

Bú shi, yǐjīng shí'èrdiǎn le.
"No, it's already twelve."

2. In each case, indicate that the correct time is two minutes earlier than the speaker says.

Xiànzài jiǔdiǎn sìshibāfēn, duì bu duì?
"It's now 9:48, right?"

Bú duì. Xiànzài jiǔdiǎn sìshiliùfēn.
"No, it's 9:46."

Xiànzài liǎngdiǎn sānshí'èrfēn, duì bu duì?
"It's now 2:32, right?"

Bú duì. Xiànzài liǎngdiǎn sānshifēn.
"No, it's 2:30."

Xiànzài sìdiǎn wǔshiliùfēn, duì bu duì?
"It's now 4:56, right?"

Bú duì. Xiànzài sìdiǎn wǔshisìfēn.
"No, it's 4:54."

Xiànzài liùdiǎn líng sānfēn, duì bu duì?
"It's now 6:03, right?"

Bú duì. Xiànzài liùdiǎn líng yīfēn.
"No, it's 6:01."

Xiànzài shídiǎn èrshi'èrfēn, duì bu duì?
"It's now 10:22, right?"

Bú duì. Xiànzài shídiǎn èrshifēn.
"No, it's 10:20."

Xiànzài shí'èrdiǎn shíyīfēn, duì bu duì?
"It's now 12:11, right?"

Bú duì. Xiànzài shí'èrdiǎn líng jiǔfēn.
"No, it's now 12:09."

3. Answer the following questions in the negative, using **kǒngpà** and adding a changed status **le** at the end.

Xiǎo Wáng lái bu lái?
"Is Little Wang coming?"

Kǒngpà tā bù láile.
"I'm afraid he's not coming."

Nǐ qù bu qù?
"Are you going?"

Kǒngpà wǒ bú qùle.
"I'm afraid I'm not going."

Tāmen mǎi bu mǎi?
"Are they going to buy it?"

Kǒngpà tāmen bù mǎile.
"I'm afraid they're not going to buy it."

Lín Lǎoshī yào bu yào?
"Does Prof. Lin want it?"

Kǒngpà tā bú yàole.
"I'm afraid she doesn't want it."

Wǒ mèimei kéyi bu kéyi lái?
"Can my sister come?"

Kǒngpà tā bù kéyi láile.
"I'm afraid your sister can't come."

4. Drop the nouns from the following phrases to create nominal phrases ending in -**de**.

shídiǎnbànde huǒchē
"the 10:30 train"

shídiǎnbànde
"the 10:30 one"

wǒ mǎide gōngshìbāo
"the briefcase that I bought"

wǒ mǎide
"the one I bought"

wǒ mèimeide dàizi
"my younger sister's bag"

wǒ mèimeide
"my younger sister's"

bānshangde nǚshēng
"the girls in the class"

bānshangde
"the ones in the class"

liǎngdiǎn zhōngde huǒchē
"the 2:00 train"

liǎngdiǎn zhōngde
"the 2:00 one"

nǐ màide bēibāo
"the backpack that you sold"

nǐ màide
"the one that you sold"

lǎoshīde míngzi
"the teacher's name"

lǎoshīde
"the teacher's"

5. When asked how many hours it will take, explain that you're afraid it will take one hour more than the speaker says.

Yào bu yào yíge zhōngtóu?
"Will it take one hour?"

Kǒngpà yào liǎngge zhōngtóu!
"I'm afraid it will take two hours!"

Yào bu yào liǎngge zhōngtóu?
"Will it take two hours?"

Kǒngpà yào sān'ge zhōngtóu!
"I'm afraid it will take three hours!"

Yào bu yào sān'ge zhōngtóu?
"Will it take three hours?"

Kǒngpà yào sìge zhōngtóu!
"I'm afraid it will take four hours!"

Yào bu yào sìge zhōngtóu?
"Will it take four hours?"

Kǒngpà yào wǔge zhōngtóu!
"I'm afraid it will take five hours!"

Yào bu yào wǔge zhōngtóu?
"Will it take five hours?"

Kǒngpà yào liùge zhōngtóu!
"I'm afraid it will take six hours!"

Yào bu yào liùge zhōngtóu?
"Will it take six hours?"

Kǒngpà yào qīge zhōngtóu!
"I'm afraid it will take seven hours!"

6. When asked how many hours it will take, explain that you think it will probably take an hour less than the speaker says.

Yào wǔge bàn zhōngtóu ma?
"Will it take five and a half hours?"

Wǒ xiǎng zhǐ yào sìge bàn zhōngtóu ba.
"I think it will only take four and a half hours."

Yào liǎngge zhōngtóu ma?
"Will it take two hours?"

Wǒ xiǎng zhǐ yào yíge zhōngtóu ba.
"I think it will only take one hour."

Yào liùge zhōngtóu ma?
"Will it take six hours?"

Wǒ xiǎng zhǐ yào wǔge zhōngtóu ba.
"I think it will only take five hours."

Yào jiǔge bàn zhōngtóu ma?
"Will it take nine and a half hours?"

Wǒ xiǎng zhǐ yào bāge bàn zhōngtóu ba.
"I think it will only take eight and a half hours."

Yào qīge zhōngtóu shíwǔfēn ma?
"Will it take seven hours and fifteen minutes?"

Wǒ xiǎng zhǐ yào liùge zhōngtóu shíwǔfēn ba.
"I think it will only take six hours and fifteen minutes."

Yào shíge zhōngtóu ma?
"Will it take ten hours?"

Wǒ xiǎng zhǐ yào jiǔge zhōngtóu ba.
"I think it will only take nine hours."

7. Convert the 24-hour clock times, as commonly employed in mainland China and Taiwan, to 12-hour clock times. Add **xiàwǔ** or **wǎnshang** as appropriate.

Xiàyítàng dào Tiānjīnde huǒchē shísāndiǎn èrshifēn kāi.
"The next train to Tianjin departs at 13:20."

Xiàyítàng dào Tiānjīnde huǒchē xiàwǔ yīdiǎn èrshifēn kāi.
"The next train to Tianjin departs at 1:20 in the afternoon."

Xiàyítàng dào Běijīngde huǒchē èrshidiǎn shífēn kāi.
"The next train to Beijing departs at 20:10."

Xiàyítàng dào Běijīngde huǒchē wǎnshang bādiǎn shífēn kāi.
"The next train to Beijing departs at 8:10 in the evening."

Xiàyítàng dào Xīnjiāpōde huǒchē shíwǔdiǎn wǔshifēn kāi.
"The next train to Singapore departs at 15:50."

Xiàyítàng dào Xīnjiāpōde huǒchē xiàwǔ sāndiǎn wǔshifēn kāi.
"The next train to Singapore departs at 3:50 in the afternoon."

Xiàyítàng dào Jiā'nádàde huǒchē èrshi'èrdiǎn sānshiwǔfēn kāi.
"The next train to Canada departs at 22:35."

Xiàyítàng dào Jiā'nádàde huǒchē wǎnshang shídiǎn sānshiwǔfēn kāi.
"The next train to Canada departs at 10:35 in the evening."

BASIC
MANDARIN
CHINESE
SPEAKING & LISTENING

PRACTICE
BOOK

disc
DIGITAL DATA
MP3
Approx. run time: 15hrs 57mins

© 2017 CORNELIUS C. KUBLER &
YANG WANG

MP3 Audio & Printable PDF Exercises

This is a FREE CD-ROM
Not to be sold separately

TUTTLE
www.tuttlepublishing.com
Produced in China

For the remaining pages of Transformation
and Response Drills
(**Unit 4, Part 1** through **Unit 10, Part 4**),
please refer to the disc.

4. Role Play Exercises
Unit 1, Part 1: Role Play Exercises

Practice these role plays in Chinese to improve your spoken fluency.

1. A: How are you?

   B: How are you?

   A: Where are you going?

   B: I'm going to the dining hall. How about you?

   A: I'm going to the library.

2. A: Hello!

   B: Hi!

   A: Where are you going?

   B: I'm going back to my dorm. And you?

   A: I'm going to take care of a little something.

3. A: Hello, how are you doing?

   B: Hi!

   A: Where are you going?

   B: I'm going to the library. How about yourself?

   A: I'm also going to the library.

4. A: Hi! Where is Wang Jingsheng going?

   B: Wang Jingsheng is going to the library.

   A: And Ke Leien?

   B: Ke Leien is also going to the library.

   A: And you?

   B: I'm returning to my dorm.

The following role plays use some of the vocabulary from the Classroom Expressions.

5. A: Good morning! How are you? Where are you going?

   B: I'm going to take care of some stuff. How about you?

   A: I'm going to the dining hall.

   B: Good, very good. Goodbye! See you tomorrow.

   A: See you tomorrow!

6. A: Good morning! How are you? Where are you going?

   B: I'm going back to my dorm.

   A: Could you say that again?

   B: I'm returning to my dormitory. How about you? Where are you going?

   A: I'm also returning to my dormitory.

Unit 1, Part 2: Role Play Exercises

Practice these role plays in Chinese to improve your spoken fluency.

1. A: How are you?

   B: How are you? I haven't seen you for a long time. How have you been?

   A: Fine, thanks. How are your mom and dad?

   B: They're both fine, thanks.

   A: I'll be going now. So long!

   B: So long!

2. A: Hi! Long time no see! How have you been?

   B: Pretty good. How have you been?

   A: Very busy.

   B: I've been very busy, too.

   (switch to another pair of students)

   A: How is your spouse?

   B: He/she's fine, thanks. How about your spouse?

   A: He/she's fine, too.

   B: I have something I have to do. I'll be going now. See you!

   A: See you!

3. A: Haven't seen you for quite a while. How have you been?

   B: I've been very busy. How have you been?

   A: I've been very busy, too. How are your spouse and children?

   B: They're all fine, thanks. How are your mom and dad?

   (switch to another pair of students)

   A: They're both fine, too.

   B: Where are you going?

   A: I'm going to the library. And you?

   B: I have something I have to do. I'll be going now…

4. A: Hi! Long time no see! How have you been?

   B: I'm very tired. How have you been?

   A: I'm also very tired.

   B: How is your mom?

   A: She's very busy.

   (switch to another pair of students)

   B: How's your dad?

   A: He's fine.

   B: Where are you going?

   A: I'm returning to my dorm. And you?

   B: I'm going to the cafeteria. I'll be going now…

   A: Bye-bye!

· ·

Unit 1, Part 3: Role Play Exercises

Practice these role plays in Chinese to improve your spoken fluency.

1. A: Hi, Old Gao, how are you? Have you been busy lately?

    B: I'm still the same as before. I'm not too busy. Little Wang, how have you been recently?

    A: Pretty good, not too busy. How have your studies been going? Is Chinese hard?

    (switch to another pair of students)

    B: My studies have been quite intense. Chinese is hard! How has your work been going?

    A: My work has lately been very busy.

    B: I have something I have to do, I'll be going now. Bye!

    A: Goodbye. See you tomorrow!

2. A: Hello, Old He!

    B: Hello, Little Zhao!

    A: How have you been doing recently?

    B: Very well, thanks. Still the same as before. How have you been?

    A: Not too well. I'm too busy.

    B: Recently, I've been very busy, too.

    (switch to another pair of students)

    A: How are your children?

    B: They're all fine. Their studies have been quite intense. How is your spouse?

    A: Fine. He/she is not too busy. Where are you going? Are you going to the library?

    B: I'm not going to the library. I'm going to the cafeteria.

    A: I'm going to the library to take care of a little something. I'll be going now.

    B: Bye-bye!

3. A: Hi, Little Wang! How have you been recently?

    B: Hi, Old Ke. I'm very sleepy. How have you been? Are you sleepy, too?

    A: I'm not sleepy. Recently I've been very busy.

    B: How are your studies going? Is Chinese hard?

    A: My studies are very intense. Chinese is very hard.

    (switch to another pair of students)

    B: Chinese is not hard, Chinese is easy! Where are you going? Back to the dorm?

    A: I'm going to the library. Are you going to the library, too?

    B: I'm not going to the library. I'm returning to the dorm. Bye!

    A: Bye! See you tomorrow!

4. A: Little He, you're very tall!

    B: I'm not tall. Old Zhao, you also are not short!

5. A: My father is very tall. Is your father tall?

    B: My father is quite short. My mother is tall.

. . . .

Unit 1, Part 4: Role Play Exercises

Practice these role plays in Chinese to improve your spoken fluency.

1. A: Mr. Lin, Mrs. Lin, welcome, welcome. Come in, come in!

   B: Mr./Miss Ke, how are you? Thank you!

   A: You're welcome. Please sit down, please sit down. Are you both well?

   B: Thank you, we're both very well. Are your parents well?

   A: They're also very well, thank you.

   B: I have a little something, I must be going now. Thank you.

   A: You're welcome. Take it easy. Goodbye!

2. A: Mr. and Mrs. Xie, welcome, welcome. Come in, come in!

   B: Mr./Ms. Wang, how are you? Thank you.

   A: Please sit down, please sit down.

   B: Thank you, thank you.

   (switch to another pair of students)

   A: Mr. and Mrs. Xie, I have a little something, I must be going now.

   B: Mr./Ms. Wang, where are you going?

   A: I'm going to take care of something. Mr. and Mrs. Xie, thank you.

   B: You're welcome. Take care. Goodbye. See you tomorrow.

3. A: Teacher Zhao, welcome, welcome. Come in, come in!

   B: Mr./Miss Gao, thank you. Long time no see.

   A: Right, long time no see. Please sit down, please sit down.

   B: Thank you. How have your studies been going? Is Chinese interesting?

   (switch to another pair of students)

   A: Chinese is too hard, it's not interesting.

   B: Mr./Miss Gao, I've gotten tired, I must be going now. Thank you.

   A: You're welcome. Take it easy. Goodbye, Teacher Zhao.

   B: Goodbye, goodbye.

4. A: Old Li, how are you? Welcome, welcome!

   B: Little Gao, how have you been lately?

   A: Pretty good. Come in, come in! Have you been well lately?

   B: Still the same as before. How are your spouse and kids? Are you all well?

   A: We're all fine. My spouse is fine. My kids are also fine.

   (switch to another pair of students)

   B: How are your studies?

   A: My studies are very intense. How about you? Is your work busy?

   B: My work is not too busy.

   A: Is your work interesting?

   B: My work is uninteresting. Little Gao, I have something, I have to go now. Thank you!

   A: You're welcome. Take it easy. Goodbye!

Unit 2, Part 1: Role Play Exercises

Practice these role plays in Chinese to improve your spoken fluency.

1. A: What's your name?

    B: My name is ___. What's your name?

    A: My name is ___.

    B: Is he a teacher?

    A: Correct, he's a Chinese language teacher.

    B: What is his name?

    A: His name is Lǐ Qún. He's Malaysian.

2. A: Excuse me, what country are you guys from?

    B: I'm Canadian. She's American. What country are you from?

    A: I'm Chinese.

    B: What's your name?

    A: My name is ___. What's your name?

    B: My name is ___.

3. A: Excuse me, are they teachers?

    B: They're classmates, not teachers.

    A: Are they all Americans?

    B: Not all are. This classmate is also American, but that classmate is Taiwanese.

4. A: Excuse me, what country are you from?

    B: I'm American, Chinese-American. How about you? What country are you from?

    A: I'm also American. *(pointing to some other students)* Are they all American?

    B: They're not all American. This classmate is American, but that classmate is Japanese.

5. A: What's the name of the Chinese language teacher?

    B: Her name is Zhāng Huìqiáng.

    A: What country is she from?

    B: She's Singaporean.

    A: How has Chinese been lately? Is it hard? Is it interesting?

    B: Chinese is not hard, it's easy. It's also very interesting.

6. A: Which classmate is Spanish?

    B: This classmate is Spanish!

7. A: Which teacher is named Yáng Pēixīn?

    B: That teacher is named Yáng Pēixīn!

Unit 2, Part 2: Role Play Exercises

Practice these role plays in Chinese to improve your spoken fluency.

1. A: I will introduce you guys. Old Wang, this is Little Li. Little Li, this is Old Wang.

    B: Little Li, how are you? Happy to meet you! Welcome to China!

    C: Old Wang, how are you? Thank you. I'm also happy to meet you.

2. A: Let me introduce you. This is my new roommate, her/his name is ___. This is my old classmate, her/his name is ___.

    B: How are you? Welcome to America!

    C: I'm happy to meet you, Mr./Ms. ___.

    B: Oh, don't address me like that! It's better if you call me Little ___.

    C: O.K. In that case, why don't you also call me Little ___.

3. A: I'm your new roommate. My name is ___. I'm happy to meet you!

    B: How are you? I'm also happy to meet you. My name is ___.

    A: Excuse me, what country are you from? Are you American?

    B: I'm not American. I'm Canadian.

4. A: Who is that?

    B: She is our new roommate, her name is Lìli.

    A: And who is he?

    B: He is our Chinese teacher, Teacher Zhāng.

    A: And who are they?

    B: They are our new classmates. You don't know them?

    A: I don't know any of them. Please introduce them to me.

5. A: Excuse me, are you Chinese?

    B: No, I'm not Chinese, I'm Japanese. Are you American?

    A: No, I'm not American, I'm Canadian.

    B: How should I address you?

    A: Oh, my name is ___. It would be best if you called me Little ___. What's your name?

    B: My name is ___. In that case, why don't you also call me Little ___.

    A: Little ___, I have a little something, I'll be leaving first now. Goodbye!

    B: I must also be leaving now. Goodbye!

6. A: Mr./Miss Zhao, how are you?

    B: Don't call me like that. Just call me Little Zhao.

    A: O.K., in that case you call me Little He, too. Little Zhao, what country are you from?

    B: I'm Chinese. So how about you? What country are you from?

    A: I'm American. Welcome to America! I'm happy to meet you!

· ·

Unit 2, Part 3: Role Play Exercises

Practice these role plays in Chinese to improve your spoken fluency.

1. A: How do you do? What's your honorable surname?

   B: My last name is ___. What is your honorable surname?

   A: My last name is ___.

   B: Excuse me, I have a little something (to do). I'll leave first. Goodbye!

   A: Goodbye!

2. A: That must be your husband/wife?

   B: No, no, he/she is not my husband/wife. He/she is my colleague.

   A: Excuse me, I have a little something (to do). I'll leave first. I'm very happy to meet you!

   B: I'm also very happy to meet you. Goodbye!

3. A: I guess that must be Madam Zhao?

   B: No, no, she's not Madam Zhao. She's my Chinese teacher. Her last name is Chen.

   A: Excuse me, I have a little something (to do). I'll leave first. I'm very happy to meet you!

   B: I'm also very happy to meet you. Goodbye!

4. A: How do you do? What's your honorable surname?

   B: My last name is ___. What is your honorable surname?

   A: My last name is ___. Mr./Ms. ___, at what organization do you work?

   B: I work at the Canadian Embassy. Mr./Ms. ___, where do you work?

   A: I now don't work anymore. I study Chinese.

   (switch to another group of students)

   B: Where are you studying Chinese?

   A: I'm studying Chinese at the Chinese University of Hong Kong.

   B: Is Chinese hard?

   A: Chinese is hard, but it's very interesting.

5. A: How do you do? What's your honorable surname?

   B: My last name is ___. What's your honorable surname?

   A: My last name is ___. Mr./Ms. ___, what country are you from? Where do you work?

   B: I'm American, I work at a company. Oh, let me introduce you. This is my husband/wife, his/her name is ___.

   (switch to another group of students)

   A: How do you do? I work at the Chinese Foreign Ministry. Where do you work?

   C: I'm a college teacher. I work at ___ College.

   A: Very happy to meet you! What is your college president's last name?

   C: Our college president is surnamed ___. Do you know him/her?

   A: I know him/her! President ___ is very good. The teachers at ___ College are also all very good!

Unit 2, Part 4: Role Play Exercises

Practice these role plays in Chinese to improve your spoken fluency.

1. A: Hello! My name is ___. Please instruct me more.

    B: My surname is ___. Sorry, I didn't bring name cards.

    A: I didn't bring name cards either.

    B: Mr./Ms. ___, where do you work?

    (switch to another pair of students)

    A: I work at Peking University. Mr./Ms. ___, where do you work?

    B: I work at Sino-American Trading Company.

    A: Mr./Ms. ___, excuse me, I have to go do something. Goodbye!

    B: Bye!

2. A: General Manager Li, this is Manager Xie from China Trading Company.

    B: Oh, welcome, welcome! My name is Li. Sorry, I didn't bring name cards.

    C: My name is Gao. I work at Sino-American University. Please give me more advice.

    B: Mr./Ms. Gao, I suppose that you must be Chinese?

    (switch to another group of students)

    C: Yes, my spouse and I are both Chinese. I suppose that you are Chinese, too?

    B: No, I'm not Chinese, I'm American, Chinese-American.

    A: Excuse me, I have to go work now. I'll leave now before you all. Goodbye!

3. A: Hello! You must be Ms. Bai from the Chinese Foreign Ministry?

    B: You made a mistake. My last name is Hou, my last name is not Bai.

    A: Oh, sorry, sorry, I got it wrong.

    B: Never mind.

    (switch to another pair of students)

    A: I suppose you must be from Spain?

    B: No, no. I'm not Spanish. I'm Canadian!

    A: Sorry, sorry. I got it wrong!

    B: Never mind. I have to be going now. Goodbye! See you tomorrow!

4. A: Who is that lady?

    B: Her last name is Luo. Her whole name is Luó Měiyún.

    A: Who is that gentleman?

    B: His last name is Shi. His full name is Shī Dàpéng.

    A: I suppose they must both be Chinese?

    B: That's incorrect, you got it wrong. Neither of them is Chinese; they're Japanese!

5. A: Let's welcome ("we welcome") Madam Wood from the British Embassy!

    B: Welcome, welcome! I suppose you must be American, too? Oh, sorry, I got that wrong!

    C: You didn't get it wrong. I work at the British Embassy, but I am American.

Unit 3, Part 1: Role Play Exercises

Practice these role plays in Chinese to improve your spoken fluency.

1. A: How many students do you have in your Chinese class?

   B: There are ten—oh, that's not right, I made a mistake. There are nine.

   A: Are they all Americans?

   B: They're not all Americans. There are six Americans, two Germans, and a Frenchman.

   (switch to another pair of students)

   A: How many male students and how many female students?

   B: Four men, five women.

   A: So, how many teachers do you have in all?

   B: In all there are two. One is a male teacher, one is a female teacher.

2. A: Excuse me, how many students do you have in your English class?

   B: In all there are six.

   A: Are they all Americans?

   B: Right, they're all Americans—oh, sorry, they're not all Americans. There's one Brit.

   (switch to another pair of students)

   A: How many male students and how many female students?

   B: Half and half. Three males, three females.

   A: So, who is your teacher? I suppose it's a female teacher?

   B: Correct, it's a female teacher. Her last name is Ramirez. She's Spanish.

3. A: How many classmates are there in your dormitory?

   B: In all there are seven. The dormitory is not big, it's very small.

   A: Are your classmates all Americans?

   B: They're not all Americans. There are 3 Americans, 3 Japanese, and 1 Singaporean.

   (switch to another pair of students)

   A: I suppose your classmates are all females?

   B: No, they're not all females. There are four males and three females.

   A: It's very interesting. Are you going back to your dorm now?

   B: No, I'm going to the library to study. Tomorrow there is a test. I'm very nervous!

4. A: How many colleagues are there in your company?

   B: In all there are eight. Four men, four women—half and half. It's a small company.

   A: So, I suppose your colleagues must all be Americans?

   B: No, they're not all Americans. There are Americans, Taiwanese, and Germans.

   (switch to another pair of students)

   A: Your company's manager is a male or a female?

   B: There's a general manager and a manager. They're both female. The general manager is German, her last name is Weiss. The manager is Taiwanese, her last name is Ma.

   A: I know Manager Ma. She is very good.

   B: Right, Manager Ma is very good. She is a very interesting person.

Unit 3, Part 2: Role Play Exercises

Practice these role plays in Chinese to improve your spoken fluency.

1. A: Is this your mother? How old is she?

    B: Let me try to think. She's forty-six this year—no, forty-seven.

    A: Oh. So I suppose this must be your father?

    B: Yes, he's forty-five years old this year.

2. A: This is your younger brother, right? He's cute. How old is he this year?

    B: He's five years old. Next month he'll be six.

    A: And this is your younger sister, right? She's cute too. How old is she?

    B: She's three years old.

3. A: Is this your older brother? How old is he?

    B: Let me try to think. He's twenty-eight this year—no, twenty-nine.

    A: Oh. So I guess this must be your older sister?

    B: Yes, it's my older sister. She's twenty-seven years old this year.

4. A: You're cute! How old are you?

    B: You try to guess!

    A: Let me try to think… I think you're seventeen!

    B: That's not right. I'm thirty-two. Am I still cute?

5. A: How old are you?

    B: I'll be twenty-one next month. How old are you?

    A: You try to guess.

    B: Twenty years old?

    A: Not correct!

    B: Nineteen years old?

    A: Also not correct! I was twenty-one last month!

6. A: I have neither an older brother nor an older sister.

    B: I have neither a younger brother nor a younger sister.

    A: But you have me, right? I'm also very cute, right?

    B: Right. I have you. You also have me. But you're not cute!

7. A: Let's go back to the dormitory, O.K.?

    B: Not good. Going back to the dormitory is uninteresting.

    A: In that case, let's go the dining hall, O.K.?

    B: Good! Too good!

· ·

Unit 3, Part 3: Role Play Exercises

Practice these role plays in Chinese to improve your spoken fluency.

1. A: Excuse me, how much is this bag?

    B: That bag is 50 dollars.

    A: Wow, that's too expensive! How much is this cup?

    B: That cup is only 15 dollars, it's very cheap.

    (switch to another pair of students)

    A: Could I have a look at it?

    B: Sure, why don't you take a look. How many do you want?

    A: I'll buy one. This is 15 dollars.

    B: O.K., thank you. Goodbye!

2. A: Excuse me, how much is that?

    B: That briefcase? Let me take a look. That briefcase is 625 dollars.

    A: Gosh, that's too expensive! Well, how much is that backpack?

    B: That backpack is only 260 dollars, it's very cheap.

    A: Could I look at it?

    B: Sure, why don't you take a look. The backpacks we sell are very good.

    (switch to another pair of students)

    A: All right, I'll buy two of them.

    B: In all it's 520 dollars.

    A: 500 dollars, O.K.?

    B: I suppose it's O.K. In all it's 500 dollars.

    A: O.K., this is 500 dollars. Thank you. Goodbye.

    B: Thank you. Goodbye!

3. A: Do you have backpacks?

    B: Backpacks we have. One backpack is 1,500 dollars.

    A: Gosh, that's too expensive!

    B: It's not expensive, it's very cheap. The backpacks we sell are very good.

    (switch to another pair of students)

    A: How much is this?

    B: That bag is only 600 dollars. How many do you want to buy?

    A: Could I take a look at it?

    B: Sure, why don't you take a look.

    A: I'll buy six of them. How much is that in all?

    B: In all it's 3,600 dollars.

4. A: How much is one cent plus five cents?

    B: One cent plus five cents is six cents.

    A: How much is 90 cents minus 10 cents?

    B: 90 cents minus 10 cents is 80 cents.

Unit 3, Part 4: Role Play Exercises

Practice these role plays in Chinese to improve your spoken fluency.

1. A: Excuse me, when does the next train to Beijing (Běijīng) depart?

   B: At 11:15. But it's now already 11:10, I'm afraid you're not going to make it.

   A: Well, how about the one after the next one?

   B: Let me take a look. The one after the next one is 12:30.

   (switch to another pair of students)

   A: All right. In that case, I'll then take the 12:30 one. How much does it cost?

   B: $28.30.

   A: How long does it take to get to Beijing?

   B: It takes about one and one-half hours.

   A: O.K., thanks.

   B: You're welcome!

2. A: Excuse me, when does the next train to Taipei (**Táiběi**) depart?

   B: At 9:30. But it's now already 9:25, I'm afraid you're not going to make it.

   A: Well, how about the one after the next one?

   B: Let me take a look. The one after the next one is 9:45.

   (switch to another pair of students)

   A: All right. In that case, I'll then take the 9:45 one. How much does it cost?

   B: Fifty dollars.

   A: How long does it take to get to Taipei?

   B: It takes about half an hour. Let me take a look: it takes only twenty-five minutes.

   A: O.K., thanks.

   B: You're welcome.

3. A: Excuse me, when does the next train to Shanghai (**Shànghǎi**) depart?

   B: At 21:05. But it's now already 21:00, I'm afraid you're not going to make it.

   A: Well, how about the one after the next one?

   B: Let me take a look. The one after the next one is 23:05.

   (switch to another pair of students)

   A: All right. In that case, I'll then take the 23:05 one. How much does it cost?

   B: $133.50.

   A: Excuse me, how long does it take to get to Shanghai?

   B: It takes about four and a half hours.

   A: O.K., thanks.

   B: You're welcome!

4. A: What time are you leaving?

   B: I'm leaving at seven.

   A: What time is it now?

   B: It's already a quarter to seven. I'm not going to make it!

· ·

Unit 4, Part 1: Role Play Exercises

Practice these role plays in Chinese to improve your spoken fluency.

1. A: Excuse me, what time every day does the library open and what time does it close?

    B: It opens at 7:30 in the morning and it closes at 11:00 at night.

    A: Is it open on Saturday and Sunday?

    B: It's open on Saturday. Sundays it's open half the day; it's open in the morning, not in the afternoon.

2. A: Excuse me, what time every day does the embassy open and what time does it close?

    B: It opens at 8:15 in the morning and it closes at 4:45 in the afternoon.

    A: Is it open on Saturday and Sunday?

    B: It's open Saturday morning. Saturday afternoon and Sunday it's closed.

    A: Thank you!

    B: Not at all.

3. A: Excuse me, what time every day does Sino-American Trading Company open?

    B: It opens at 9:15 every morning; it closes at 5:30 every afternoon.

4. A: What time do you usually get up in the morning?

    B: I usually get up at 6:30 in the morning.

    A: What time do you usually go to bed at night?

    B: I usually go to bed at 11:45 at night.

5. A: How many hours do you usually sleep every day?

    B: I usually sleep seven hours a day. How about you?

    A: I usually sleep five hours a day.

    B: You only sleep five hours? Aren't you sleepy?

    A: I'm very sleepy!

6. A: How many hours do you usually sleep every day?

    B: Monday to Friday I sleep four hours a day. Saturday and Sunday I sleep ten hours a day. How about you?

    A: Monday to Friday I sleep three hours a day. Saturday and Sunday I sleep twelve hours a day.

7. A: Last Monday I was still in China!

    B: Last Tuesday I was still in Germany!

    A: Next Thursday I'm going to Japan!

    B: Next Friday I'm going to Taiwan!

Unit 4, Part 2: Role Play Exercises

Practice these role plays in Chinese to improve your spoken fluency.

1. A: What's your name?

   B: My name is ___.

   A: Which year were you born?

   B: In 1992, it's the 81st year of the Republic.

   A: Which month and which day?

   B: May 16.

   A: Your address is?

   B: Peace Road, Section Three, Lane 5, Alley 8, Number 66, 2nd Floor.

   A: O.K., please wait for a second.

2. A: What's your name? Where were you born?

   B: My name is ___. I was born in Canada.

   A: What year were you born?

   B: In 1987, it's the 76th year of the Republic.

   A: Which month and which day?

   B: November 2.

   A: Your address is?

   B: Beijing West Road, Section One, Lane 20, Alley 4, Number 5, 5th Floor.

   A: All right, please wait a minute.

3. A: Your birthday is which month and which day?

   B: My birthday is June 10. When is your birthday?

   A: My birthday is December 25.

   B: This year I'm 19. How old are you this year?

   A: This year I'm 18.

4. A: What month and day is it today? What day of the week?

   B: Today is ___.

   A: What was the date yesterday and what day of the week was it?

   B: Yesterday was ___.

   A: And what's the date tomorrow, and what day of the week?

   B: Tomorrow is ___.

5. A: What year is it this year?

   B: This year is ___.

   A: What year was it last year?

   B: Last year was ___.

   A: What year will it be next year?

   B: Next year will be ___.

· ·

Unit 4, Part 3: Role Play Exercises

Practice these role plays in Chinese to improve your spoken fluency.

1. A: Hello!

    B: Hi! Are you American?

    A: Yes, I'm an American.

    B: Is this your first trip to China?

    A: No, this is my third time. The year before last I came once, and last year I came once.

    (switch to another pair of students)

    B: How long are you going to stay this time?

    A: About two weeks. I go back to my country on November 23.

    B: What room are you staying in?

    A: I'm staying in 702.

    B: Oh, sorry, I have to go now. Goodbye!

    A: Goodbye!

2. A: Hello! I suppose you must be Chinese?

    B: Yes, I'm Chinese.

    A: Welcome to America!

    B: Thank you.

    A: Is this your first trip to the States?

    B: No, this is my fourth time. I came twice last year, once in 1989, and once in 1998.

    (switch to another pair of students)

    A: How long are you going to stay this time?

    B: About a month and a half. I go back on February 15th.

    A: What room are you staying in?

    B: I'm staying in 428.

    A: Nice meeting you!

    B: I'm glad to have met you, too!

3. A: Have you ever taken a train before?

    B: I've taken a train before. And you?

    A: I've never taken a train before.

4. A: Have you ever been to Malaysia before?

    B: I've been to Singapore, but I haven't been to Malaysia. How about you?

    A: Singapore, Malaysia, I've been to both.

5. A: Are you returning home tomorrow?

    B: Yes, I'm returning home tomorrow at noon. How about you? I suppose you're going home also?

    A: I've been too busy recently, this time I'm not returning home.

Unit 4, Part 4: Role Play Exercises

Practice these role plays in Chinese to improve your spoken fluency.

1. A: Excuse me, what's the population of China?

   B: China has about one billion 300 million people.

   A: What's the population of Taiwan?

   B: Taiwan has more than 20 million people.

2. A: Excuse me, what's the population of Hong Kong?

   B: Hong Kong has about seven million people.

   A: Well, and what's the population of Singapore?

   B: Singapore's population is comparatively small. It seems it only has about 5 million people.

   A: Oh, Singapore only has 5 million people?

   B: That's right!

3. A: Excuse me, what's the population of America?

   B: America has almost 300 million people.

   A: What's the population of England?

   B: England has more than 60 million people.

   A: Well, and what about Canada?

   B: Canada's population is comparatively small. It seems it only has 32 million people.

4. A: Excuse me, what's the population of Shanghai?

   B: Shanghai's people are very many. Shanghai has about 17 million people!

   A: What's the population of Guangzhou?

   B: Guangzhou's population is comparatively smaller. It seems it has more than 9 million people.

5. A: Excuse me, what's the population of Xi'an?

   B: Xi'an has about 8 million people.

   A: Well, and what about Taipei?

   B: The population of Taipei is comparatively small. It seems it only has about 3 million people.

6. A: What days of the week do you have Chinese class?

   B: We have Chinese class every day.

   A: Do you often skip class?

   B: I don't skip class.

   A: Have you ever been late for class?

   B: I've been late for class two or three times.

. . . .

Unit 5, Part 1: Role Play Exercises

Practice these role plays in Chinese to improve your spoken fluency.

1. A: Excuse me, I'd like to find Mrs. Li. Is she here?

   B: Which Mrs. Li?

   A: I'm really sorry, I don't know her Chinese name. However, her English name is Gertrude.

   B: Gertrude? Oh, I know now. Her Chinese name is Lǐ Gē. But, you know, she's not here right now!

   (switch to another pair of students)

   A: Do you know where she is now?

   B: It seems she's now in the general manager's office.

   A: In that case, could I leave her a note?

   B: Of course you can.

   A: Thank you.

2. A: Come in!

   B: Excuse me, I'd like to find Mr. Wang. Is he here?

   A: Mr. Wang? Which Mr. Wang?

   B: I'm really sorry, I'm American, and my Chinese is not too good. I don't know his Chinese name. But his English name is Hank.

   A: Hank Wang? Oh, I know now. His Chinese name is Wáng Jiànjūn. But, you know, he's not here right now!

   (switch to another pair of students)

   B: Do you know where Mr. Wang is right now?

   A: It seems he's now in the college president's office.

   B: In that case, could I leave him a note?

   A: Of course you can.

   B: Thank you.

3. A: Excuse me, if Little Xie isn't there, what should I do?

   B: You could leave a note for her.

4. A: The chairs are here. But where's the table?

   B: The table is over there.

   A: Oh, that's right. Thank you!

5. A: I'd like to buy this chair and that table.

   B: You're only buying one chair?

   A: Yes. How much is this chair? And how much is that table?

   B: This chair costs $200. That table costs $500. In all that's $700.

   A: All right. Thank you. Goodbye.

Unit 5, Part 2: Role Play Exercises

Practice these role plays in Chinese to improve your spoken fluency.

1. A: Excuse me, is there anybody in this seat?

    B: No, there isn't. Go ahead and sit down.

    A: Do you often come here to eat?

    B: No, I don't come often. How about you?

    (switch to another pair of students)

    A: I eat here often. I come almost every day.

    B: Are you a student?

    A: Yes. Are you a student, too?

    B: No, I'm a laborer. I work at Nanjing Shoe Factory No. 13.

2. A: Anybody in this seat?

    B: No. Have a seat!

    A: Do you often come here to eat breakfast?

    B: No, I don't come often. How about you?

    A: I also don't come often. Are you a student?

    B: No, I work in a trading company. How about you?

    (switch to another pair of students)

    A: I'm a college student in America. This year I'm studying Chinese in China.

    B: Where are you studying Chinese?

    A: At Peking University's Chinese Language Training Center. Gosh! It will soon be 9:00. I have to go to attend class. Bye!

    B: Goodbye!

3. A: I'm a student. I study English at Taiwan University. I suppose you're a student too?

    B: No, I'm not a student. I'm already over 30! I work at a company.

4. A: Excuse me, where do you usually eat?

    B: I usually eat in the college dining hall. It's comparatively cheap.

5. A: Breakfast, lunch, and dinner, do you eat them all in the university dining hall?

    B: Lunch and dinner I eat at the dining hall. I don't eat breakfast.

6. A: Have you ever eaten Chinese food?

    B: Chinese food, I've eaten it very many times.

    A: Do you like to eat Chinese food?

    B: I very much like to eat Chinese food.

    A: In that case, today's lunch, we'll eat Chinese food, O.K.?

    B: That's too good!

Unit 5, Part 3: Role Play Exercises

Practice these role plays in Chinese to improve your spoken fluency.

1. A: Excuse me, where's the bathroom?

   B: It's over there.

2. A: I want to find the bathroom. Excuse me, where's the bathroom?

   B: It's over there—sorry, I made a mistake, it's over here.

3. A: Old Bai, sorry to have made you wait so long.

   B: It's nothing, it's nothing. Old Li, long time no see! You've really gotten thinner!

   A: On this trip of yours to Shanghai, where are you staying?

   B: I'm staying at the Shanghai Hotel, Room 107. Do you still live where you lived before?

   (switch to another pair of students)

   A: No, the year before last we moved to Pǔdōng.

   B: Where is Pǔdōng?

   A: Pǔdōng is to the west of Shanghai. And you? Are you still living in the same place?

   B: In March of this year we moved to the south of the United States.

4. A: Little Zhang, sorry to have made you wait so long.

   B: Never mind. Old Chen, long time no see! You really have put on some weight!

   A: You've put on some weight, too. Both of us have gotten fatter!

   (switch to another pair of students)

   A: On this trip of yours to Tianjin, where are you staying?

   B: I'm staying at the Tianjin Hotel, Room 227. Do you still live where you lived before?

   A: Correct, we still live in the same place as before. We welcome you to come!

5. A: (You) look! That child is really too fat!

   B: That child is too fat? That child is mine. Your children are not thin either!

6. A: Where is my cup? I have to find my cup!

   B: O.K. We'll first look over here, and then we'll go there and look.

7. A: In which part of China is Chéngdū?

   B: Chéngdū is in the west of China.

8. A: Excuse me, in which part of China is Guǎngxī?

   B: Guǎngxī is in the south of China. Guǎngxī is to the west of Guǎngdōng, which is to say that Guǎngdōng is to the east of Guǎngxī.

Unit 5, Part 4: Role Play Exercises

Practice these role plays in Chinese to improve your spoken fluency.

1. A: Yesterday I bought a new computer. It's in my study. Do you want to see it?

    B: All right! It's a Pentium, right? Inside it, how much RAM is there?

    A: Of course it's a Pentium. Inside it, there are 64 megabytes.

    B: I suppose the switch ought to be in front?

    (switch to another pair of students)

    A: No, the switch is in the back.

    B: Could I see the operating manual?

    A: Of course you can. However, there is only a Chinese one, there is no English one.

    B: Never mind. Where is the operating manual?

    (switch to another pair of students)

    A: It's on the table to the left—no, it's on the chair to the right—I'm sorry, I made a mistake, it's on the computer!

    B: O.K. Hey, what is that thing under the table?

    A: Oh, it's Lassie (**Láixǐ**), our family's dog. Don't pay any attention to her.

    B: I very much love dogs! Lassie, come!

2. A: The day before yesterday I bought a new computer. It's in my room. You want to see it?

    B: Of course I want to see it! It's a Pentium, right? Inside it, how much RAM is there?

    A: Of course it's a Pentium. Inside it, there are 128 megabytes.

    B: Where is the switch? I suppose the switch ought to be in back?

    A: No, this is a new computer. The switch is on top.

    (switch to another pair of students)

    B: On top? That's interesting! Could I see the operating manual?

    A: Of course you can. It's on the bookcase to the right—no, it's on the table to the left—I'm sorry, I don't know where it is.

    B: In that case, I will go look for it. Oh, who is that little kid?

    A: That's my two-year old little brother. Just ignore him.

    B: He's really cute!

3. A: How much does this computer cost?

    B: This computer costs $1,000.

    A: And how much does that computer cost?

    B: That computer costs $1,500.

    A: Both are new computers, right?

    B: They're not new ones, but they're very good. Do you want to take a look?

    A: They're not new ones? If I buy computers, of course I buy new ones! I'm leaving!

    B: Don't leave! Do you want to see our new computers? Don't leave, don't leave!

4. A: Excuse me, was Old Zhao there?

    B: No, Old Zhao was not there, but I left a note.

Unit 6, Part 1: Role Play Exercises

Practice these role plays in Chinese to improve your spoken fluency.

1. A: Uncle, how are you?

    B: How are you, little friend! What's your name? How old are you?

    A: My name is Lùlu. I'm 7.

    B: Lùlu, I guess you already go to elementary school?

    (switch to another group of students)

    A: Yes, I go to second grade.

    B: This is a little present I'm giving you.

    A: Thank you, uncle.

    B: You're welcome.

    A: Mm, it tastes really good!

2. A: Auntie, how are you?

    B: How are you? What's your name?

    A: My name is Xiǎo Míng.

    B: How old are you, Xiǎo Míng? I suppose you already go to elementary school?

    A: I'm five years old. I don't go to school yet.

    B: Xiǎo Míng, this is candy I'm giving you.

    A: I very much like to eat candy. Thank you, Auntie!

3. A: Do you like dogs?

    B: I very much like little dogs. They're cute!

    A: Do you like me?

    B: I don't like you. You're not cute!

4. A: What year in college are you?

    B: I'm a senior. How about you? What year in college are you?

    A: I'm a junior. My younger brother is a sophomore, my younger sister is a first-year.

5. A: Let me introduce a friend to you. This is Little Ma. Little Ma, this is Little Ke.

    B: Little Ke, I'm happy to meet you!

    C: Little Ma, I'm also happy to meet you!

6. A: Excuse me, have you ever eaten Chinese food?

    B: I've eaten Chinese food before. It's delicious. I very much like to eat Chinese food.

7. A: Does she have a boyfriend?

    B: She has two boyfriends. One is good-looking, one is not too good-looking.

Unit 6, Part 2: Role Play Exercises

Practice these role plays in Chinese to improve your spoken fluency.

1. A: Hi! Are you Chinese?

    B: Yes, I'm Chinese.

    A: What place in China?

    B: I was born in Tianjin, and then I grew up in Beijing. Where are you from?

    A: I'm from Canada. You look quite young. I guess you're not yet 20?

    B: I'm 19. I'll be 20 next month.

2. A: How are you? Are you American?

    B: No, I'm German.

    A: What place in Germany?

    B: I was born in Berlin (**Bólín**), and I grew up in Hamburg (**Hànbǎo**). Where are you from?

    A: I'm from Shanghai. You look quite young. I guess you're not yet 30?

    B: I'm 24. I'll be 25 in April.

3. A: Where were you born?

    B: I was born in New York and then I grew up in San Francisco.

    A: Interesting! I was born in San Francisco and then I grew up in New York.

4. A: Are you married?

    B: I'm already married.

    A: Do you have kids?

    B: We have three children, one son and two daughters. How about you? Are you married?

    A: I'm a college student. I haven't yet gotten married.

5. A: What are you doing sitting there?

    B: May I not sit here?

    A: I didn't say you may not sit there! I asked you what you are doing sitting there.

6. A: Moving is very tiring! Have you ever moved?

    B: I have moved before; I have moved twice.

7. A: What is the food in the dining hall like? Does it taste good?

    B: The dining hall food, in looking at it it looks tasty, but in eating it it's not very tasty.

8. A: Excuse me, what is the meaning of **shémme dìfang**?

    B: The meaning of **shémme dìfang** is **nǎr**. I suppose now you understand?

Unit 6, Part 3: Role Play Exercises

Practice these role plays in Chinese to improve your spoken fluency.

1. A: Are you married? Do you have kids?

   B: I'm married. I have two kids, a son and a daughter.

   A: How old are your children? Are they already in school?

   B: They're still too small. My son is five and my daughter is ten months old, so they're not in school yet.

   (switch to another group of students)

   A: Where do you work?

   B: I serve at Northwest Airlines.

   A: Oh. Does your spouse work also?

   B: He/she teaches at a high school. However, because our children are still small, he/she only can work half days.

2. A: Are you married? Do you have kids?

   B: I'm married. I have a daughter.

   A: How old is your daughter? I suppose she is already in school?

   B: Yes, she's already attending school. She's seven years old and is already in second grade in elementary school.

   (switch to another group of students)

   A: Where do you work?

   B: I work at Southwest Airlines.

   A: Oh. Does your spouse work also?

   B: He/she works at a trading company. However, because our daughter is still small, he/she only can work half days.

   A: This is a small present that I am giving your daughter. It's candy. There are no children that don't like to eat candy!

3. A: Excuse me, what's your name? Where do you work?

   B: My name is ___. I teach at a junior high school.

   A: What do you teach?

   B: I teach English.

4. A: What time every morning does your mother go to work?

   B: She goes to work every morning at 9:00 A.M.

   A: What time every afternoon does she get off from work?

   B: She gets off from work every afternoon at 5:00 P.M.

5. A: Why do many people say that Chinese is hard to learn?

   B: I think it's because Chinese characters are too many. Chinese characters are also hard to write, right?

Unit 6, Part 4: Role Play Exercises

Practice these role plays in Chinese to improve your spoken fluency.

1. A: Do you have any brothers or sisters?

   B: I have one older brother and one younger brother. How about you?

   A: I have two older sisters and one younger sister.

   B: Oh, it's already 9:00! Sorry, I have something I have to do, I'll be going first now. In the future, when there's a chance, why don't we chat again!

2. A: Do you have any siblings?

   B: I'm the oldest in our family. I have two younger brothers and two younger sisters. How about you? Do you have any brothers or sisters?

   A: I have two older sisters and one younger sister.

   B: Oh, it's already 10:00. I have to go to class. I've already been late too many times! In the future, when there's a chance, let's chat again!

3. A: How many brothers and sisters do you have?

   B: I'm the second oldest in our family. I have an older sister and a younger brother.

   A: Where do your sister and brother live? Do they live in America?

   B: No. My older sister immigrated to England. My little brother is studying abroad in China.

4. A: How many brothers and sisters do you have?

   B: I have one older brother, one younger brother, one older sister, and one younger sister.

   A: Do they all live in China?

   B: My parents, older brother, and younger brother live in China. My older sister immigrated to Canada; she got married to a Canadian. My younger sister is studying abroad in Japan.

5. A: Oh, sorry. I forgot to introduce myself. My name is ___.

   B: My name is ___. This is my name card, please instruct me much.

   A: Thank you, thank you. Sorry, I forgot to carry name cards.

   B: That's O.K. Sorry, I have a little something, I have to leave first. In the future when there's a chance, let's chat again.

6. A: How are you? This is my name card. My name is ___.

   B: Thank you, thank you. Sorry, I forgot to introduce myself. My name is ___. I was born in Beijing and grew up in Shanghai. I also will give you a name card.

   A: You were born in Beijing and grew up in Shanghai? Very interesting! I was born in Shanghai and grew up in Beijing.

   B: Right, very interesting. O.K., nice to meet you. Excuse me, I have something I have to do. In the future when there's a chance, let's chat again! I much enjoy chatting with friends.

For the remaining pages of Role Play Exercises
(**Unit 7, Part 1** through **Unit 10, Part 4**),
please refer to the disc.

5. Listening Comprehension Exercises

Unit 1, Part 1: Listening Comprehension Exercises

NAME _____ COURSE _____ DATE _____

Based on the recorded passages, circle the best response to each of the questions that follows. You may listen to each passage as many times as needed.

EXERCISE ONE: QUESTIONS

1. **Where is the female speaker going?**

    (A) To the dorm

    (B) To the dining hall

    (C) To do something

2. **Where is the male speaker going?**

    (A) To the dorm

    (B) To the dining hall

    (C) To do something

EXERCISE TWO: QUESTIONS

1. **Where is the male speaker going?**

    (A) To the dorm

    (B) To the library

    (C) To the dining hall

2. **Where is the female speaker going?**

    (A) To the dorm

    (B) To the library

    (C) To the dining hall

3. **What is the name of the female speaker?**

    (A) Wang Jingsheng

    (B) Zhang Taisheng

    (C) Jia Aihua

Unit 1, Part 2: Listening Comprehension Exercises

NAME _____ COURSE _____ DATE _____

Based on the recorded passages, circle the best response to each of the questions that follows. You may listen to each passage as many times as needed.

EXERCISE ONE: QUESTIONS

1. **How has the female speaker been?**

    (A) She is fine.

    (B) She is busy.

    (C) She is tired.

2. **Where is the male speaker going?**

    (A) He is going to the library.

    (B) He is going to the dining hall.

    (C) He is going to the dorm.

EXERCISE TWO: QUESTIONS

1. **How are the female speaker's spouse and child?**

    (A) They are fine.

    (B) They are busy.

    (C) They are tired.

2. **How are the male speaker's parents?**

    (A) They are fine.

    (B) They are busy.

    (C) They are tired.

3. **Where is the male speaker going?**

    (A) To the dining hall

    (B) To the library

    (C) To do something

Unit 1, Part 3: Listening Comprehension Exercises

NAME _____   COURSE _____   DATE _____

Based on the recorded passages, circle the best response to each of the questions that follows. You may listen to each passage as many times as needed.

EXERCISE ONE: QUESTIONS

1. **How has Old Gao been recently?**

   (A) Very tired

   (B) Very nervous

   (C) The same as before

2. **How are his children doing?**

   (A) They are fine.

   (B) They are tired.

   (C) They are busy with their studies.

EXERCISE TWO: QUESTIONS

1. **What is the relationship between the two speakers?**

   (A) Husband and wife

   (B) Teacher and student

   (C) Colleagues

2. **What does the female speaker think about the Chinese language?**

   (A) It's easy to learn.

   (B) It's difficult to learn.

   (C) It's neither easy nor difficult to learn.

3. **Where is the female speaker going?**

   (A) Dorm

   (B) Library

   (C) Cafeteria

Unit 1, Part 4: Listening Comprehension Exercises

NAME _____   COURSE _____   DATE _____

Based on the recorded passages, circle the best response to each of the questions that follows. You may listen to each passage as many times as needed.

EXERCISE ONE: QUESTIONS

1. **How are the female speaker's husband and children?**

    (A) They are fine.

    (B) They are busy.

    (C) They are tired.

2. **How are the male speaker's parents?**

    (A) They are fine.

    (B) They are busy.

    (C) They are the same as before.

EXERCISE TWO: QUESTIONS

1. **What does the female speaker ask the male speaker to do?**

    (A) To come in

    (B) To sit down

    (C) To speak Chinese

2. **How has the female speaker been?**

    (A) She has been fine.

    (B) She has been busy.

    (C) She has been tired.

3. **What does the female speaker think about the Chinese language?**

    (A) Chinese is easy and interesting.

    (B) Chinese is difficult but interesting.

    (C) Chinese is difficult and not interesting.

Unit 2, Part 1: Listening Comprehension Exercises

NAME _____ COURSE _____ DATE _____

Based on the recorded passages, circle the best response to each of the questions that follows. You may listen to each passage as many times as needed.

EXERCISE ONE: QUESTIONS

1. **What is the nationality of the speaker's father?**

   (A) American

   (B) Canadian

   (C) Japanese

2. **What is the nationality of the speaker's mother?**

   (A) American

   (B) Canadian

   (C) Japanese

EXERCISE TWO: QUESTIONS

1. **What is the name of the female speaker?**

   (A) Ke Jingling

   (B) Ke Jinling

   (C) Ke Jinlin

2. **What is the nationality of the female speaker?**

   (A) Singaporean

   (B) American

   (C) Spanish

3. **What is the nationality of the female speaker's spouse?**

   (A) Singaporean

   (B) American

   (C) Spanish

Unit 2, Part 2: Listening Comprehension Exercises

NAME _____ COURSE _____ DATE _____

Based on the recorded passages, circle the best response to each of the questions that follows. You may listen to each passage as many times as needed.

EXERCISE ONE: QUESTIONS

1. **Who is the person that the two speakers are discussing?**

    (A) The male speaker's new teacher

    (B) The male speaker's new roommate

    (C) The male speaker's old friend

2. **What is the nationality of the person that the two speakers are talking about?**

    (A) American

    (B) Spanish

    (C) Canadian

EXERCISE TWO: QUESTIONS

1. **What is Zhang Tianming's nationality?**

    (A) Chinese

    (B) American

    (C) Spanish

2. **Where did this conversation take place?**

    (A) Taipei

    (B) Shanghai

    (C) Beijing

3. **By what name does the female speaker prefer to be called?**

    (A) Miss Wang

    (B) Xiao Wang

    (C) Lili

Unit 2, Part 3: Listening Comprehension Exercises

NAME _____ COURSE _____ DATE _____

Based on the recorded passages, circle the best response to each of the questions that follows. You may listen to each passage as many times as needed.

EXERCISE ONE: QUESTIONS

1. **Where does the female speaker work?**

    (A) The Chinese Embassy

    (B) A company

    (C) A university

2. **Where does the male speaker work?**

    (A) The American Embassy

    (B) A company

    (C) A university

EXERCISE TWO: QUESTIONS

1. **Who is the person being discussed?**

    (A) Teacher Wang's mother

    (B) Teacher Wang's colleague

    (C) Teacher Wang's wife

2. **What is this person's surname?**

    (A) Wang

    (B) Li

    (C) Zhang

3. **What does this person teach?**

    (A) Chinese

    (B) English

    (C) Japanese

Unit 2, Part 4: Listening Comprehension Exercises

NAME _____ COURSE _____ DATE _____

Based on the recorded passages, circle the best response to each of the questions that follows. You may listen to each passage as many times as needed.

EXERCISE ONE: QUESTIONS

1. **Where does the female speaker work?**

    (A) Embassy

    (B) University

    (C) Trading company

2. **Where does the male speaker work?**

    (A) Embassy

    (B) University

    (C) Trading company

EXERCISE TWO: QUESTIONS

1. **What does the speaker's husband do?**

    (A) He is a college student.

    (B) He is the general manager of a company.

    (C) He is a university professor.

2. **What is the speaker's nationality?**

    (A) British

    (B) Malaysian

    (C) Japanese

3. **What is the nationality of the speaker's husband?**

    (A) American

    (B) Chinese

    (C) British

Unit 3, Part 1: Listening Comprehension Exercises

NAME _____ COURSE _____ DATE _____

Based on the recorded passages, circle the best response to each of the questions that follows. You may listen to each passage as many times as needed.

EXERCISE ONE: QUESTIONS

1. **How many Chinese language teachers does the female speaker have?**

    (A) Three

    (B) Four

    (C) Five

2. **How many of her teachers are American?**

    (A) One

    (B) Two

    (C) Three

3. **How many of her teachers are male?**

    (A) Two

    (B) Three

    (C) Four

EXERCISE TWO: QUESTIONS

1. **How many Japanese students are there in the male speaker's class?**

    (A) One

    (B) Two

    (C) Five

2. **How many female students are there in his class?**

    (A) Three

    (B) Six

    (C) Nine

Unit 3, Part 2: Listening Comprehension Exercises

NAME _____   COURSE _____   DATE _____

Based on the recorded passages, circle the best response to each of the questions that follows. You may listen to each passage as many times as needed.

EXERCISE ONE: QUESTIONS

1. **Who is the person being talked about?**

    (A) The female speaker's brother

    (B) The female speaker's older sister

    (C) The female speaker's younger sister

2. **How old is this person now?**

    (A) 5

    (B) 6

    (C) 7

EXERCISE TWO: QUESTIONS

1. **How old is the male speaker's father?**

    (A) 63

    (B) 54

    (C) 47

2. **Where does the male speaker's father work?**

    (A) A company

    (B) A university

    (C) An embassy

3. **How old is the male speaker's youngest brother?**

    (A) 8

    (B) 9

    (C) 10

Unit 3, Part 3: Listening Comprehension Exercises

NAME _____   COURSE _____   DATE _____

Based on the recorded passages, circle the best response to each of the questions that follows. You may listen to each passage as many times as needed.

EXERCISE ONE: QUESTIONS

1. **What does the female speaker want to buy?**

    (A) A cup

    (B) A bag

    (C) A briefcase

2. **How much does it cost?**

    (A) 500 RMB

    (B) 520 RMB

    (C) 1000 RMB

EXERCISE TWO: QUESTIONS

1. **What does the male speaker want to buy?**

    (A) A cup

    (B) A backpack

    (C) A briefcase

2. **How many does he want to buy?**

    (A) One

    (B) Three

    (C) Five

3. **How much is he going to pay?**

    (A) 15 RMB

    (B) 40 RMB

    (C) 45 RMB

Unit 3, Part 4: Listening Comprehension Exercises

NAME _____ COURSE _____ DATE _____

Based on the recorded passages, circle the best response to each of the questions that follows. You may listen to each passage as many times as needed.

EXERCISE ONE: QUESTIONS

1. **How has the male speaker been?**

    (A) He has been busy.

    (B) He has been tired.

    (C) He has been sleepy.

2. **What time does the conversation take place?**

    (A) About 5:15

    (B) About 6:30

    (C) About 6:45

EXERCISE TWO: QUESTIONS

1. **When is the male speaker going to take the train to Taipei?**

    (A) 3:10

    (B) 3:15

    (C) 5:30

2. **How long does it take to get to Taipei by train?**

    (A) About three hours

    (B) About four hours

    (C) About ten hours

3. **How much does the train ticket cost?**

    (A) 285 NT

    (B) 665 NT

    (C) 685 NT

Unit 4, Part 1: Listening Comprehension Exercises

NAME _____ COURSE _____ DATE _____

Based on the recorded passages, circle the best response to each of the questions that follows. You may listen to each passage as many times as needed.

EXERCISE ONE: QUESTIONS

1. **What time does the language lab open on Saturday?**

    (A) 8:30 A.M.

    (B) 9:30 A.M.

    (C) 10:30 A.M.

2. **What time does the language lab close on Wednesday?**

    (A) 8:30 P.M.

    (B) 9:30 P.M.

    (C) 10:30 P.M.

EXERCISE TWO: QUESTIONS

1. **What year in college is the speaker?**

    (A) Freshman

    (B) Sophomore

    (C) Junior

2. **When does the speaker usually get up every day?**

    (A) 6:30 A.M.

    (B) 7:30 A.M.

    (C) 8:30 A.M.

3. **How many hours of sleep does the speaker usually get every day?**

    (A) Six hours

    (B) Seven hours

    (C) Eight hours

4. **When does the speaker go to study at the library?**

    (A) Monday to Friday

    (B) Monday to Thursday

    (C) Almost every day

Unit 4, Part 2: Listening Comprehension Exercises

NAME _____   COURSE _____   DATE _____

Based on the recorded passages, circle the best response to each of the questions that follows. You may listen to each passage as many times as needed.

EXERCISE ONE: QUESTIONS

1. **When is the male speaker's birthday?**

   (A) August 31, 1986

   (B) July 17, 1987

   (C) August 31, 1987

2. **What does the male speaker do in Beijing?**

   (A) Working

   (B) Teaching

   (C) Studying

3. **What is the male speaker's address?**

   (A) 213, Building 14, Peking University

   (B) 321, Building 15, Peking University

   (C) 213, Building 15, Peking University

EXERCISE TWO: QUESTIONS

1. **When did this conversation take place?**

   (A) March 13

   (B) March 14

   (C) March 15

2. **How old is the female speaker now?**

   (A) 20 years old

   (B) 21 years old

   (C) 22 years old

Unit 4, Part 3: Listening Comprehension Exercises

NAME _____ COURSE _____ DATE _____

Based on the recorded passages, circle the best response to each of the questions that follows. You may listen to each passage as many times as needed.

EXERCISE ONE: QUESTIONS

1. **When did the female speaker first come to China?**

    (A) This year

    (B) Last year

    (C) The year before last

2. **When does the female speaker plan to return to her country?**

    (A) April

    (B) August

    (C) December

EXERCISE TWO: QUESTIONS

1. **What is Li Weijian's nationality?**

    (A) Chinese

    (B) American

    (C) Japanese

2. **How many times has Li Weijian been to China?**

    (A) One time

    (B) Two times

    (C) Three times

3. **When does Li Weijian plan to return to his country?**

    (A) October

    (B) November

    (C) December

Unit 4, Part 4: Listening Comprehension Exercises

NAME_____ COURSE_____ DATE_____

Based on the recorded passages, circle the best response to each of the questions that follows. You may listen to each passage as many times as needed.

EXERCISE ONE: QUESTIONS

1. **What is the approximate population of England?**

   (A) 30,000,000

   (B) 60,000,000

   (C) 80,000,000

2. **What is the population of Shanghai?**

   (A) More than 13,000,000

   (B) More than 15,000,000

   (C) More than 18,000,000

3. **About how many more people does Shanghai have than Beijing?**

   (A) 3,000,000

   (B) 4,000,000

   (C) 5,000,000

EXERCISE TWO: QUESTIONS

1. **What is the approximate population of Hong Kong?**

   (A) 5,600,000

   (B) 6,500,000

   (C) 6,800,000

2. **What is the approximate population of Taipei?**

   (A) 3,000,000

   (B) 4,000,000

   (C) 5,000,000

3. **How many times has the male speaker been to Taipei?**

   (A) About 10 times

   (B) About 20 times

   (C) About 30 times

Unit 5, Part 1: Listening Comprehension Exercises

NAME _____ COURSE _____ DATE _____

Based on the recorded passages, circle the best response to each of the questions that follows. You may listen to each passage as many times as needed.

EXERCISE ONE: QUESTIONS

1. **What is the last name of the person the male speaker is looking for?**

   (A) Wàn

   (B) Wáng

   (C) Wāng

2. **Where is the person that the male speaker is looking for?**

   (A) At the person's own office

   (B) At Teacher Zhang's office

   (C) At the female speaker's office

3. **Where is the male speaker from?**

   (A) Taiwan

   (B) Mainland China

   (C) U.S.

EXERCISE TWO: QUESTIONS

1. **Where is Li Derong?**

   (A) At home

   (B) At his office

   (C) At the manager's office

2. **Why did the male speaker call?**

   (A) Because he wants to buy 150 tables and 250 chairs.

   (B) Because he wants to buy 250 tables and 150 chairs.

   (C) Because he wants to buy 250 tables and 50 chairs.

Unit 5, Part 2: Listening Comprehension Exercises

NAME _____ COURSE _____ DATE _____

Based on the recorded passages, circle the best response to each of the questions that follows. You may listen to each passage as many times as needed.

EXERCISE ONE: QUESTIONS

1. **Where is the speaker studying this year?**
    (A) Chinese high school
    (B) Peking University
    (C) Language center

2. **Where will the speaker go next year?**
    (A) Hong Kong
    (B) Beijing
    (C) The United States

3. **Which meals did the speaker eat in the dining hall last year?**
    (A) Breakfast
    (B) Lunch
    (C) Breakfast, lunch, and dinner

4. **Which meals does the speaker eat in the dining hall now?**
    (A) Breakfast
    (B) Lunch
    (C) Breakfast, lunch, and dinner

EXERCISE TWO: QUESTIONS

1. **What are the two speakers doing?**
    (A) Having breakfast
    (B) Having lunch
    (C) Having dinner

2. **Does the male speaker come to the restaurant often?**
    (A) Yes, often
    (B) No, not often
    (C) He has only been once

3. **How many times has the female speaker been to the restaurant?**
    (A) One time
    (B) Two times
    (C) Three times

4. **Where does the male speaker work?**
    (A) At a university
    (B) At a factory
    (C) At a company

. . . .

Unit 5, Part 3: Listening Comprehension Exercises

NAME _____   COURSE _____   DATE _____

Based on the recorded passages, circle the best response to each of the questions that follows. You may listen to each passage as many times as needed.

EXERCISE ONE: QUESTIONS

1. **What is the female speaker's hotel room number?**

    (A) 58

    (B) 158

    (C) 258

2. **How long does the female speaker plan to stay?**

    (A) Half a month

    (B) One month

    (C) A month and a half

3. **What does the female speaker do when the male speaker says she has lost weight?**

    (A) She ignores him.

    (B) She disagrees with him.

    (C) She explains why.

EXERCISE TWO: QUESTIONS

1. **How many times has the female speaker been to China?**

    (A) One time

    (B) Two times

    (C) She has never been.

2. **How many times has the male speaker been to China?**

    (A) One time

    (B) Two times

    (C) He has never been.

3. **Where is Suzhou?**

    (A) To the north of Shanghai

    (B) To the east of Shanghai

    (C) To the west of Shanghai

Unit 5, Part 4: Listening Comprehension Exercises

NAME_____   COURSE_____   DATE_____

Based on the recorded passages, circle the best response to each of the questions that follows. You may listen to each passage as many times as needed.

EXERCISE ONE: QUESTIONS

1. **When did the male speaker buy the iPhone?**

    (A) The day before yesterday

    (B) Yesterday

    (C) Today

2. **Where is the iPhone now?**

    (A) On the bookshelf behind the female speaker

    (B) On the table to the right of the female speaker

    (C) On the table to the left of the female speaker

3. **Where is the instruction manual now?**

    (A) On the right of the iPhone

    (B) On the left of the iPhone

    (C) Next to the iPhone

EXERCISE TWO: QUESTIONS

1. **Where is the backpack?**

    (A) On the bookshelf in the study

    (B) On the table in the study

    (C) Next to the computer

2. **Where is the instruction manual?**

    (A) To the right of the bookshelf

    (B) On the bookshelf to the right

    (C) On the bookshelf to the left

3. **What is the main topic of this dialog?**

    (A) A backpack

    (B) A computer

    (C) An instruction booklet

Unit 6, Part 1: Listening Comprehension Exercises

NAME_____ COURSE_____ DATE_____

Based on the recorded passages, circle the best response to each of the questions that follows. You may listen to each passage as many times as needed.

EXERCISE ONE: QUESTIONS

1. **When was the speaker born?**

    (A) 1993

    (B) 1994

    (C) 1995

2. **What is the speaker's current year in school?**

    (A) Second year of junior high school

    (B) Third year of junior high school

    (C) First year of senior high school

3. **What did the speaker receive for his birthday?**

    (A) A backpack

    (B) A computer

    (C) A bookshelf

EXERCISE TWO: QUESTIONS

1. **What year in college is the female speaker's child?**

    (A) First year

    (B) Second year

    (C) Third year

2. **What do we know about the woman whom the female speaker would like to introduce to the male speaker?**

    (A) She works at a trading company.

    (B) She is a colleague of the female speaker's husband.

    (C) She is 26 years old.

3. **Based on the dialog, which of the following statements is NOT true?**

    (A) The male speaker is older than the female speaker.

    (B) The female speaker is married.

    (C) The female speaker has lost some weight.

Unit 6, Part 2: Listening Comprehension Exercises

NAME_____   COURSE_____   DATE_____

Based on the recorded passages, circle the best response to each of the questions that follows. You may listen to each passage as many times as needed.

EXERCISE ONE: QUESTIONS

1. **Where did the female speaker grow up?**

    (A) Hong Kong

    (B) New York

    (C) San Francisco

2. **How old is the female speaker?**

    (A) 18

    (B) 19

    (C) 20

3. **How many siblings does the female speaker have?**

    (A) 1

    (B) 2

    (C) 3

EXERCISE TWO: QUESTIONS

1. **Where does Zhang Guoshu's ex-wife work?**

    (A) High school

    (B) University

    (C) Company

2. **Where does Zhang Guoshu's current wife work?**

    (A) High school

    (B) University

    (C) Company

3. **How old is Zhang Guoshu's daughter?**

    (A) Two

    (B) Five

    (C) Twelve

Unit 6, Part 3: Listening Comprehension Exercises

NAME _____   COURSE _____   DATE _____

Based on the recorded passages, circle the best response to each of the questions that follows. You may listen to each passage as many times as needed.

EXERCISE ONE: QUESTIONS

1. **At the beginning of the dialog, what is the first speaker's problem?**

    (A) He missed class.

    (B) He ate too much food.

    (C) He's late to an appointment.

2. **What is the problem with this place?**

    (A) It's hard to find.

    (B) It's too expensive.

    (C) There are too many students.

3. **Why didn't Mr. Bai come?**

    (A) His children are still small.

    (B) He is busy with his studies.

    (C) He has things to do at home.

4. **What is one aspect of Chinese that the first speaker says is hard to learn?**

    (A) Culture

    (B) Grammar

    (C) Computer input

EXERCISE TWO: QUESTIONS

1. **What city is the speaker's husband from?**

    (A) Shanghai

    (B) Tianjin

    (C) Pudong

2. **Where is Pudong?**

    (A) In the northeast of Shanghai

    (B) In the northwest of Shanghai

    (C) In the southeast of Shanghai

3. **How old is the speaker's daughter?**

    (A) Ten months old

    (B) Five years old

    (C) Eight years old

4. **Where does the speaker's husband work?**

    (A) University

    (B) Trade company

    (C) Airline

Unit 6, Part 4: Listening Comprehension Exercises

NAME _____ COURSE _____ DATE _____

Based on the recorded passages, circle the best response to each of the questions that follows. You may listen to each passage as many times as needed.

EXERCISE ONE: QUESTIONS

1. **How many sisters does the male speaker have?**

   (A) One

   (B) Two

   (C) Three

2. **Where did the speaker grow up?**

   (A) New York

   (B) Los Angeles

   (C) Guangzhou

3. **Where do his maternal grandparents parents live?**

   (A) New York

   (B) Los Angeles

   (C) Guangzhou

EXERCISE TWO: QUESTIONS

1. **What is the age of the female speaker relative to her siblings?**

   (A) Eldest

   (B) Second eldest

   (C) Third eldest

2. **Where is the female speaker's brother?**

   (A) China

   (B) United States

   (C) England

3. **When did the female speaker go to the United States?**

   (A) Two years ago

   (B) One year ago

   (C) Two months ago

Unit 7, Part 1: Listening Comprehension Exercises

NAME _____ COURSE _____ DATE _____

Based on the recorded passages, circle the best response to each of the questions that follows. You may listen to each passage as many times as needed.

EXERCISE ONE: QUESTIONS

1. **Who are the people in the picture?**

    (A) The female speaker's sister and her family

    (B) The female speaker's cousin and her family

    (C) The female speaker's aunt and her family

2. **What does the woman in the picture do for a living?**

    (A) Factory work

    (B) Business

    (C) Teaching

EXERCISE TWO: QUESTIONS

1. **Where does the female speaker live now?**

    (A) To the northeast of Beijing

    (B) To the northwest of Beijing

    (C) To the southeast of Beijing

2. **Where does the female speaker's son go to school now?**

    (A) Elementary school

    (B) Junior high school

    (C) Senior high school

3. **Where does the female speaker's husband work?**

    (A) Kindergarten

    (B) Elementary school

    (C) Junior high school

Unit 7, Part 2: Listening Comprehension Exercises

NAME _____ COURSE _____ DATE _____

Based on the recorded passages, circle the best response to each of the questions that follows. You may listen to each passage as many times as needed.

EXERCISE ONE: QUESTIONS

1. **Where is the female speaker studying now?**

   (A) United States

   (B) Mainland China

   (C) Taiwan

2. **How many characters does the female speaker know?**

   (A) One hundred

   (B) Seven hundred

   (C) Several hundred

3. **What other foreign language has the female speaker learned?**

   (A) French

   (B) Japanese

   (C) Spanish

EXERCISE TWO: QUESTIONS

1. **Where did the female speaker learn English?**

   (A) Elementary school

   (B) Junior high school

   (C) University

2. **For how long did the female speaker learn English?**

   (A) Half a year

   (B) A year and a half

   (C) Eight years

3. **What does the female speaker think of English?**

   (A) It's easy.

   (B) It's hard.

   (C) It's interesting.

4. **For how long did the female speaker learn Spanish?**

   (A) Half a year

   (B) A year and a half

   (C) Eight years

Unit 7, Part 3: Listening Comprehension Exercises

NAME _____ COURSE _____ DATE _____

Based on the recorded passages, circle the best response to each of the questions that follows. You may listen to each passage as many times as needed.

EXERCISE ONE: QUESTIONS

1. **In which month did the male speaker arrive in Hong Kong?**

    (A) January

    (B) February

    (C) March

2. **How long did the male speaker learn Chinese?**

    (A) Less than a year

    (B) A year

    (C) More than a year

3. **What level is the Chinese of the male speaker's wife?**

    (A) Beginning

    (B) Advanced

    (C) She speaks no Chinese.

EXERCISE TWO: QUESTIONS

1. **Where is Nanjing?**

    (A) In the south of China

    (B) In the east of China

    (C) In the northwest of China

2. **In what level of school is the speaker?**

    (A) Junior high school

    (B) Senior high school

    (C) University

3. **With whom did the speaker come to the U.S.?**

    (A) Sister

    (B) Brother

    (C) Cousin

4. **What criticism does the speaker express?**

    (A) Chinatown is dirty.

    (B) New Yorkers talk too fast.

    (C) New York is very expensive.

. . . .

Unit 7, Part 4: Listening Comprehension Exercises

NAME _____ COURSE _____ DATE _____

Based on the recorded passages, circle the best response to each of the questions that follows. You may listen to each passage as many times as needed.

EXERCISE ONE: QUESTIONS

1. **What did the male speaker do after graduating from college?**

    (A) Teach school.

    (B) Go to graduate school.

    (C) Work at a trading company.

2. **What does the female speaker want to do after graduating from college?**

    (A) Teach school.

    (B) Go to graduate school.

    (C) Work at a trading company.

3. **What is NOT said about the city of Harbin?**

    (A) It is cold.

    (B) It is a good area.

    (C) The people there are nice.

EXERCISE TWO: QUESTIONS

1. **How long did the female speaker study in Beijing?**

    (A) Four months

    (B) Six months

    (C) Ten months

2. **What are the male speaker's future plans?**

    (A) Go to graduate school in the U.S.

    (B) Go to graduate school in China

    (C) Study in China for a couple of years

3. **What is NOT said about Beijing?**

    (A) The air is bad.

    (B) The traffic is congested.

    (C) There isn't much crime.

For the remaining pages of
Listening Comprehension Exercises
(**Unit 8, Part 1** through **Unit 10, Part 4**),
please refer to the disc.

6. Dictation Exercises

Dictation Exercise 1

PRONUNCIATION AND ROMANIZATION: INITIALS

NAME _____ COURSE _____ DATE _____

Based on the recording for this exercise, write in the correct Pinyin initials. The finals and tones are indicated. You may listen to the recording as many times as needed.

1. _____ā   11. _____ēn   21. _____uē

2. _____ū   12. _____uī   22. _____ēng

3. _____ī   13. _____ān   23. _____ōng

4. _____ō   14. _____ū   24. _____uān

5. _____āi   15. _____ū   25. _____uān

6. _____iā   16. _____ē   26. _____āng

7. _____ōu   17. _____ā   27. _____uī

8. _____āo   18. _____ī   28. _____ā

9. _____iē   19. _____ī   29. _____āo

10. _____īn   20. _____iān   30. _____ī

Dictation Exercise 2

PRONUNCIATION AND ROMANIZATION: FINALS

NAME _____ COURSE _____ DATE _____

Based on the recording for this exercise, write in the correct Pinyin finals, which are all in Tone One. The initials are indicated. You may listen to the recording as many times as needed.

1. f _____   11. r _____   21. y_____

2. j _____   12. g _____   22. z_____

3. t _____   13. w _____   23. q _____

4. x_____   14. l _____   24. r _____

5. j _____   15. zh_____   25. n _____

6. c_____   16. b _____   26. j _____

7. sh _____   17. x_____   27. q _____

8. y_____   18. m _____   28. s_____

9. z_____   19. k_____   29. z_____

10. ch _____   20. p _____   30. zh_____

· ·

Dictation Exercise 3

PRONUNCIATION AND ROMANIZATION: TONES

NAME _____ COURSE _____ DATE _____

Based on the recording for this exercise, add the correct Pinyin tones. The initials and finals are indicated. You may listen to the recording as many times as needed.

1. ta _____	11. zhi _____	21. xue _____
2. ma _____	12. shu _____	22. lan _____
3. wo _____	13. tan _____	23. mai _____
4. shei _____	14. lü _____	24. mai _____
5. hao _____	15. lu _____	25. pai _____
6. lei _____	16. ru _____	26. er _____
7. sha _____	17. rou _____	27. xiu _____
8. gui _____	18. lüe _____	28. shuo _____
9. ni _____	19. ku _____	29. kuang _____
10. mei _____	20. li _____	30. feng _____

Dictation Exercise 4

PRONUNCIATION AND ROMANIZATION: INITIALS, FINALS, AND TONES

NAME _____ COURSE _____ DATE _____

Based on the recording for this exercise, write the initial, final, and tone for the syllables you hear. You may listen to the recording as many times as needed.

1. _____

2. _____

3. _____

4. _____

5. _____

6. _____

7. _____

8. _____

9. _____

10. _____

11. _____

12. _____

13. _____

14. _____

15. _____

16. _____

17. _____

18. _____

19. _____

20. _____

21. _____

22. _____

23. _____

24. _____

25. _____

26. _____

27. _____

28. _____

29. _____

30. _____

. . . .

Dictation Exercise 5

CLASSROOM EXPRESSIONS 1–32

NAME _____   COURSE _____   DATE _____

Based on the recording for this exercise, write below the English equivalents for the Chinese expressions you hear. Note that some of the classroom expressions from the textbook have here been combined or slightly rearranged. You may listen to the recording as many times as needed.

1. _____   11. _____

2. _____   12. _____

3. _____   13. _____

4. _____   14. _____

5. _____   15. _____

6. _____   16. _____

7. _____   17. _____

8. _____   18. _____

9. _____   19. _____

10. _____   20. _____

Dictation Exercise 6

UNIT 3, PART 2: NUMBERS 1–99 AND AGES

NAME _____ COURSE _____ DATE _____

Based on the recording for this exercise, write the number or age that you hear (in the case of ages, write "___ years old"). You may listen to the recording as many times as needed.

1. _____   11. _____   21. _____

2. _____   12. _____   22. _____

3. _____   13. _____   23. _____

4. _____   14. _____   24. _____

5. _____   15. _____   25. _____

6. _____   16. _____   26. _____

7. _____   17. _____   27. _____

8. _____   18. _____   28. _____

9. _____   19. _____   29. _____

10. _____   20. _____   30. _____

Dictation Exercise 7

UNIT 3, PART 3: NUMBERS 1–9,999 AND MONEY AMOUNTS

NAME _____   COURSE _____   DATE _____

Based on the recording for this exercise, write the number or money amount that you hear (in the case of money amounts, assume it is American money and indicate $ or ¢ as appropriate). You may listen to the recording as many times as needed.

1. _____   11. _____   21. _____

2. _____   12. _____   22. _____

3. _____   13. _____   23. _____

4. _____   14. _____   24. _____

5. _____   15. _____   25. _____

6. _____   16. _____   26. _____

7. _____   17. _____   27. _____

8. _____   18. _____   28. _____

9. _____   19. _____   29. _____

10. _____   20. _____   30. _____

Dictation Exercise 8

UNIT 3, PART 4: CLOCK TIMES AND AMOUNTS OF TIME

NAME _____ COURSE _____ DATE _____

Based on the recording for this exercise, write the clock time or amount of time that you hear. (Write clock times as hour followed by minutes, e.g., "5:35"; indicate amounts of time with "hours" or "minutes", e.g., "2 hours" or "10 minutes.") You may listen to the recording as many times as needed.

1. _____   11. _____   21. _____

2. _____   12. _____   22. _____

3. _____   13. _____   23. _____

4. _____   14. _____   24. _____

5. _____   15. _____   25. _____

6. _____   16. _____   26. _____

7. _____   17. _____   27. _____

8. _____   18. _____   28. _____

9. _____   19. _____   29. _____

10. _____   20. _____   30. _____

Dictation Exercise 9

UNIT 4, PART 2: DATES

NAME_____ COURSE_____ DATE_____

Based on the recording for this exercise, write the date that you hear, including day of the week, month, day of the month, and year. For example, if you hear the Chinese for "Monday, July 4, 2011," then write below in this order and with these abbreviations: "Mon., 7/4/2011." You may listen to the recording as many times as needed.

1._____   11._____

2._____   12._____

3._____   13._____

4._____   14._____

5._____   15._____

6._____   16._____

7._____   17._____

8._____   18._____

9._____   19._____

10._____   20._____

Dictation Exercise 10

UNIT 4, PART 4: LARGE NUMBERS

NAME _____ COURSE _____ DATE _____

Based on the recording for this exercise, write numerically the number that you hear as it would be written in the U.S. For example, for "one billion three hundred million," write "1,300,000,000." If the Chinese uses **duō** to indicate "more than," then use a plus mark (+) after the number. You may listen to the recording as many times as needed.

1. _____   11. _____   21. _____

2. _____   12. _____   22. _____

3. _____   13. _____   23. _____

4. _____   14. _____   24. _____

5. _____   15. _____   25. _____

6. _____   16. _____   26. _____

7. _____   17. _____   27. _____

8. _____   18. _____   28. _____

9. _____   19. _____   29. _____

10. _____   20. _____   30. _____

7. Translation Exercises for Each Part (Lesson)

. . . .

Unit 1, Part 1: Translation Exercise

NAME _____ COURSE _____ DATE _____

Translate the following sentences into Pinyin romanization with correct tone marks. If you have forgotten a word, consult the English-Chinese Glossary in the back of your textbook.

1. Where is Ke Leien going?

2. I'm going to the cafeteria. How about you?

3. Wang Jingsheng is going back to the dorm.

4. Ke Leien is going to take care of some things.

5. You're going to the library; I also am going to the library.

Unit 1, Part 2: Translation Exercise

NAME _____ COURSE _____ DATE _____

Translate the following sentences into Pinyin romanization with correct tone marks. If you have forgotten a word, consult the English-Chinese Glossary in the back of your textbook.

1. I'm tired; are you tired, too?

2. Haven't seen you for a long time! Are you busy?

3. He is busy; his wife and children are also all busy.

4. How have your mom and dad been? Are they both well?

5. She has a little something (she has to do); I also have a little something (I have to do).

Unit 1, Part 3: Translation Exercise

NAME _____ COURSE _____ DATE _____

Translate the following sentences into Pinyin romanization with correct tone marks. If you have forgotten a word, consult the English-Chinese Glossary in the back of your textbook.

1. Chinese is not hard; Chinese is easy!

2. Little Wang, hi! How have you been lately?

3. Recently her studies have not been too intense.

4. Recently we have all been quite busy. (use tǐng...-de pattern)

5. Is Old Zhao going? Are you going? (use affirmative-negative question pattern)

Unit 1, Part 4: Translation Exercise

NAME _____   COURSE _____   DATE _____

Translate the following sentences into Pinyin romanization with correct tone marks. If you have forgotten a word, consult the English-Chinese Glossary in the back of your textbook.

1. Teacher Wang, please come in! Please sit down!

2. We've gotten tired. Have you (plural) **gotten tired, too?**

3. A: Ms. Gao, thank you! B: You're welcome. Take care!

4. Mr. Li, how are you? Mrs. Li, how are you? (be as polite as possible)

5. Miss Lin, I have a little something (I have to do); I must be going now. Goodbye!

· ·

Unit 2, Part 1: Translation Exercise

NAME_____   COURSE_____   DATE_____

Translate the following sentences into Pinyin romanization with correct tone marks. If you have forgotten a word, consult the English-Chinese Glossary in the back of your textbook.

1. She is American, Chinese-American. How about you?

2. Are both of you Chinese? And how about that classmate?

3. Excuse me, what country are you from? Are you Japanese? (be polite)

4. I'm called (write your own Chinese surname and given name). **What's your name?**

5. They're not all good fathers. This teacher is a good father, but that teacher isn't a good father.

. . . .

Unit 2, Part 2: Translation Exercise

NAME _____　COURSE _____　DATE _____

Translate the following sentences into Pinyin romanization with correct tone marks. If you have forgotten a word, consult the English-Chinese Glossary in the back of your textbook.

1. We welcome you to come to America! (be polite)

2. Who is your (plural) **teacher? Who are your classmates?**

3. Welcome! Please come in, please sit down. Don't leave!

4. I'm happy to meet you. Excuse me, how should I address you?

5. Don't address me like this. It would be better if you called me Little Gao.

. . . .

Unit 2, Part 3: Translation Exercise

NAME_____ COURSE_____ DATE_____

Translate the following sentences into Pinyin romanization with correct tone marks. If you have forgotten a word, consult the English-Chinese Glossary in the back of your textbook.

1. I study at Taiwan University; where do you study?

2. This person must be your spouse, I suppose? (be polite)

3. My mother works at a company. Where does your mother work?

4. Mr. Wu works at the Foreign Ministry, Mrs. Wu works at the Japanese Embassy.

5. What is your last name? At which organization do you work? (be as polite as you can)

Unit 2, Part 4: Translation Exercise

NAME _____ COURSE _____ DATE _____

Translate the following sentences into Pinyin romanization with correct tone marks. If you have forgotten a word, consult the English-Chinese Glossary in the back of your textbook.

1. Sorry, I didn't go, I also didn't ask.

2. None of them went to the dining hall.

3. A: Have they come? B: They still haven't come.

4. Not all of them are Chinese, but none of us are Canadians.

5. Miss Wang from the Chinese Embassy has come. Do you know her?

· ·

Unit 3, Part 1: Translation Exercise

NAME _____ COURSE _____ DATE _____

Translate the following sentences into Pinyin romanization with correct tone marks. If you have forgotten a word, consult the English-Chinese Glossary in the back of your textbook.

1. We in the class have nine classmates. (be polite)

2. You guys in all have how many Chinese language teachers?

3. One is a male student, eight are female students. (no need to be polite)

4. In the class there are seven French people, six Chinese people, and four Germans.

5. There are five teachers; two are male teachers, three are female teachers. (be polite)

. . . .

Unit 3, Part 2: Translation Exercise

NAME _____   COURSE _____   DATE _____

Translate the following sentences into Pinyin romanization with correct tone marks. If you have forgotten a word, consult the English-Chinese Glossary in the back of your textbook.

1. How old is their child?

2. Next month I'll be 19 years old.

3. How old is your mother this year?

4. You don't have an older brother, right?

5. Let me try to think: My father is 61 this year.

. . . .

Unit 3, Part 3: Translation Exercise

NAME _____ COURSE _____ DATE _____

Translate the following sentences into Pinyin romanization with correct tone marks. If you have forgotten a word, consult the English-Chinese Glossary in the back of your textbook.

1. Why don't we buy one, too?

2. How much does that backpack cost?

3. The cups and bags she sells are all too expensive.

4. Why don't you take a look. This is very good, also very inexpensive.

5. This briefcase costs three thousand four hundred and fifty-nine dollars.

Unit 3, Part 4: Translation Exercise

NAME _____ COURSE _____ DATE _____

Translate the following sentences into Pinyin romanization with correct tone marks. If you have forgotten a word, consult the English-Chinese Glossary in the back of your textbook.

1. In that case, I then will take the 10:00 train.

2. We will take the 9:30 one. How about you?

3. To Tianjin it takes about one and one-half hours.

4. Excuse me, how long does it take to get to Singapore?

5. Now it's already 2:30; I'm afraid you guys are not going to make it.

Unit 4, Part 1: Translation Exercise

NAME _____ COURSE _____ DATE _____

Translate the following sentences into Pinyin romanization with correct tone marks. If you have forgotten a word, consult the English-Chinese Glossary in the back of your textbook.

1. Excuse me, is the library open on Sunday?

2. I ordinarily sleep seven hours every day. How about you?

3. Monday, Wednesday, Friday the company is open half the day.

4. I usually get up at 7:00 in the morning and go to sleep at 11:00 at night.

5. The language lab opens at 9:00 in the morning, and closes at 8:30 in the evening.

Unit 4, Part 2: Translation Exercise

NAME _____ COURSE _____ DATE _____

Translate the following sentences into Pinyin romanization with correct tone marks. If you have forgotten a word, consult the English-Chinese Glossary in the back of your textbook.

1. Her mother's birthday is November 24.

2. His father was born on September 19, 1965 in England.

3. What is the date tomorrow and what day of the week is it?

4. My address is Peace Road, Section 3, Lane 46, Alley 5, Number 27, 7th floor.

5. How many days? One day! How many weeks? Two weeks! How many months? Three months! How many years? Four years!

· ·

Unit 4, Part 3: Translation Exercise

NAME _____   COURSE _____   DATE _____

Translate the following sentences into Pinyin romanization with correct tone marks. If you have forgotten a word, consult the English-Chinese Glossary in the back of your textbook.

1. This is my third time in China.

2. Teacher Wang this year went twice.

3. On November 25th I'll be going home.

4. I've never been (= "gone") to China before. Have you been there before?

5. A: How long will you be staying? B: This time I want to stay one month.

Unit 4, Part 4: Translation Exercise

NAME _____   COURSE _____   DATE _____

Translate the following sentences into Pinyin romanization with correct tone marks. If you have forgotten a word, consult the English-Chinese Glossary in the back of your textbook.

1. How many people are there in Shanghai?

2. Taiwan has about twenty-four million people.

3. It seems Taipei only has three million people.

4. It seems Guangzhou has more than twelve million people.

5. Guangzhou's population is comparatively larger. (use **duō** "be many, much")

. . . .

Unit 5, Part 1: Translation Exercise

NAME _____ COURSE _____ DATE _____

Translate the following sentences into Pinyin romanization with correct tone marks. If you have forgotten a word, consult the English-Chinese Glossary in the back of your textbook.

1. Where is that table?

2. Do you know where that chair is?

3. Excuse me, is Ms. Zhang present?

4. If I'm not there, can you leave me a note?

5. Mrs. Zhang is here, but Ms. Zhang is not here now.

Unit 5, Part 2: Translation Exercise

NAME _____ COURSE _____ DATE _____

Translate the following sentences into Pinyin romanization with correct tone marks. If you have forgotten a word, consult the English-Chinese Glossary in the back of your textbook.

1. I work there.

2. Where do you eat breakfast?

3. We often come here to eat Chinese food.

4. She is studying Chinese language at Peking University.

5. Gosh! Soon it will be seven o'clock. I have to go eat dinner!

Unit 5, Part 3: Translation Exercise

NAME _____ COURSE _____ DATE _____

Translate the following sentences into Pinyin romanization with correct tone marks. If you have forgotten a word, consult the English-Chinese Glossary in the back of your textbook.

1. Shanghai is in the east of China.

2. The year before last they moved to Chengdu.

3. Little Li, you really have gotten a little fatter!

4. I'm looking for the toilet; excuse me, where's the toilet?

5. This time I'm staying at the Beijing Hotel. Where do you live?

Unit 5, Part 4: Translation Exercise

NAME _____ COURSE _____ DATE _____

Translate the following sentences into Pinyin romanization with correct tone marks. If you have forgotten a word, consult the English-Chinese Glossary in the back of your textbook.

1. In the cup there are five cents.

2. The computer is on that table to your right.

3. The switch is not in the front, it's in the back.

4. That thing that is on top—don't concern yourself with it!

5. Little Wang is outside the library; he's not inside the library.

Unit 6, Part 1: Translation Exercise

NAME _____ COURSE _____ DATE _____

Translate the following sentences into Pinyin romanization with correct tone marks. If you have forgotten a word, consult the English-Chinese Glossary in the back of your textbook.

1. That is the candy that she gave me.

2. Auntie, let me introduce a friend to you.

3. The dining hall food is not very good to eat.

4. This is a little present that I'm giving you. (be polite)

5. Her boyfriend is already in his senior year; he's quite good-looking.

. . . .

Unit 6, Part 2: Translation Exercise

NAME_____ COURSE_____ DATE_____

Translate the following sentences into Pinyin romanization with correct tone marks. If you have forgotten a word, consult the English-Chinese Glossary in the back of your textbook.

1. Little Jin, you look very sleepy!

2. I'm not yet married. Are you married?

3. Excuse me, what does qiānzhèng mean?

4. Old Sun, I suppose you're not yet fifty years old?

5. My Chinese friend was born in Tianjin and then grew up in Beijing.

. . . .

Unit 6, Part 3: Translation Exercise

NAME _____   COURSE _____   DATE _____

Translate the following sentences into Pinyin romanization with correct tone marks. If you have forgotten a word, consult the English-Chinese Glossary in the back of your textbook.

1. That child is six months old.

2. Why do you only work half the day?

3. Do you like to teach? What do you teach?

4. Because we're very busy, we didn't wait for him.

5. You work at Northeast Airlines, right? When do you go to work and when do you get off from work?

Unit 6, Part 4: Translation Exercise

NAME _____ COURSE _____ DATE _____

Translate the following sentences into Pinyin romanization with correct tone marks. If you have forgotten a word, consult the English-Chinese Glossary in the back of your textbook.

1. He's the oldest in their family.

2. Sorry, I forgot to introduce myself.

3. Mrs. Zhang, in the future if there is an opportunity, let's chat again!

4. I have one older sister and one younger brother. How many siblings do you have?

5. My older brother is studying abroad in Japan; my younger sister immigrated to France.

. . . .

Unit 7, Part 1: Translation Exercise

NAME _____ COURSE _____ DATE _____

Translate the following sentences into Pinyin romanization with correct tone marks. If you have forgotten a word, consult the English-Chinese Glossary in the back of your textbook.

1. Who all is there in their family?

2. My parents used to work in a factory. ("used to" = "formerly")

3. Formerly I sold computers; now I've changed my line of work.

4. She works in a kindergarten; she has to go to work at 7:00 in the morning.

5. Because his health is not too good, therefore he now is not engaged in business anymore.

Unit 7, Part 2: Translation Exercise

NAME _____ COURSE _____ DATE _____

Translate the following sentences into Pinyin romanization with correct tone marks. If you have forgotten a word, consult the English-Chinese Glossary in the back of your textbook.

1. I can speak a little Chinese, but (I) speak it not too well.

2. She only knows English, she can't speak other languages.

3. I recognize about two hundred Chinese characters; some I can write, others I can't.

4. He used to be able to write Chinese characters, but now he has completely forgotten.

5. Oh, your Chinese characters are written not badly! (indicate this is something obvious)

. . . .

Unit 7, Part 3: Translation Exercise

NAME _____ COURSE _____ DATE _____

Translate the following sentences into Pinyin romanization with correct tone marks. If you have forgotten a word, consult the English-Chinese Glossary in the back of your textbook.

1. No wonder the things here are so expensive!

2. I didn't come alone. I came together with my parents.

3. We arrived this year in September. When did you arrive?

4. Sometimes I go with my classmates, sometimes I go alone.

5. My Chinese in the beginning was learned in America, later I studied for a while in China.

. . . .

Unit 7, Part 4: Translation Exercise

NAME _____ COURSE _____ DATE _____

Translate the following sentences into Pinyin romanization with correct tone marks. If you have forgotten a word, consult the English-Chinese Glossary in the back of your textbook.

1. I hear you speak English very well.

2. Six months ago I couldn't yet speak Chinese.

3. Little Gao, where did you study before you came here?

4. In 3 months, we're going to China for study abroad. ("in 3 months" = "after 3 months")

5. In China the great majority of people start working after they graduate from high school.

For the remaining pages of Translation Exercises:
For Each Part (Lesson)
(**Unit 8, Part 1** through **Unit 10, Part 4**),
please refer to the disc.

8. Translation Exercises for Each Complete Unit

Unit 1: Translation Exercise

NAME_____ COURSE_____ DATE_____

Translate the following sentences into Pinyin romanization with correct tone marks. If you have forgotten a word, consult the English-Chinese Glossary in the back of your textbook.

1. Teacher Zhao is very good; he is very interesting.

2. Chinese is not too hard, and it's also not too easy.

3. Miss Ke, welcome! Please come in, please sit down.

4. Mrs. Li, has your work been busy recently? (be polite)

5. I'm going to take care of some things. How about you?

6. She is very tall; her mom and dad are also both very tall.

7. I'll go to the library; you please go back to the dormitory.

8. We have all gotten tired. Have you (plural) **also gotten tired?**

9. I have a little something to do; I must be going now. Goodbye!

10. Little Lin, how are you? Long time no see! Where are you going?

Unit 2: Translation Exercise

NAME _____ COURSE _____ DATE _____

Translate the following sentences into Pinyin romanization with correct tone marks. If you have forgotten a word, consult the English-Chinese Glossary in the back of your textbook.

1. I know Ms. Ma from the U.S. Embassy.

2. I suppose your studies must be very intense.

3. General Manager He, welcome to America! (be polite)

4. A: Sorry, I got it wrong, I didn't bring name cards. B: Never mind.

5. Excuse me, who is that? What's his name? What unit does he work in?

6. Don't address me like that. It would be better if you called me Little Wu.

7. My mother and I work at a trading company, my dad doesn't work anymore.

8. I will introduce you: this gentleman is my new colleague; his last name is Bai.

9. Old Wang, don't go back to the dining hall. It would be better if you went to the library.

10. They're my classmates; they're not all Americans. Little Lin is Chinese; she's very busy.

Unit 3: Translation Exercise

NAME _____ COURSE _____ DATE _____

Translate the following sentences into Pinyin romanization with correct tone marks. If you have forgotten a word, consult the English-Chinese Glossary in the back of your textbook.

1. How much is nine plus eight minus six?

2. This bag is cheap. Why don't you buy one too?

3. I don't have an older brother, also don't have an older sister.

4. In our Chinese class, in all there are twelve classmates, right?

5. This one costs $4,000, that one costs $5,000. Too expensive!

6. Would it be all right if I took a look at your name card? Thanks!

7. I'm afraid the classmate who works in the library is no longer coming.

8. Let me try to think... My mom will be forty-seven years old next month.

9. My mom and dad are coming at 11:45; it will still take an hour and a half.

10. A: How much does that cup cost? B: This cup only costs two dollars and ninety-eight cents.

• •

Unit 4: Translation Exercise

NAME _____ COURSE _____ DATE _____

Translate the following sentences into Pinyin romanization with correct tone marks. If you have forgotten a word, consult the English-Chinese Glossary in the back of your textbook.

1. She was born in Taipei on July 23, 1995.

2. This is the third time that he's going to China.

3. It seems Hong Kong has more than seven million people.

4. It seems yesterday was October 17, a Wednesday. Is that right?

5. This is my second time here; this time I'm going to stay for three months.

6. That trading company is open half-days on Saturdays; it's closed on Sundays.

7. The library opens daily at 8:45 in the morning and closes at 7:30 in the evening.

8. I've been to Shanghai, but I've never been to Guangzhou. Have you been there?

9. The first person wants to go for one day; the second person wants to go for one year.

10. Her address is 6th Floor, No. 108, Alley 22, Lane 345, Nanjing East Road Section Three.

Unit 5: Translation Exercise

NAME _____ COURSE _____ DATE _____

Translate the following sentences into Pinyin romanization with correct tone marks. If you have forgotten a word, consult the English-Chinese Glossary in the back of your textbook.

1. If you're tired, you may sleep here.

2. Little Sun, do you know where the boss is?

3. Miss Zhang was not in. I left her a message.

4. Is she also studying Chinese at Peking University?

5. Last year they moved to Tianjin; it's east of Beijing.

6. Next month Mrs. Chen is coming here to study English.

7. The dog was on the bookshelf, the child was under the table.

8. This computer is a little cheaper, that computer is a little more expensive.

9. It will soon be 12:00. The shoe factory workers will soon be eating lunch.

10. A: Where does Mr. Bai live? B: He lives in Nanjing, to the west of Shanghai.

Unit 6: Translation Exercise

NAME_____ COURSE_____ DATE_____

Translate the following sentences into Pinyin romanization with correct tone marks. If you have forgotten a word, consult the English-Chinese Glossary in the back of your textbook.

1. I'm a first-year and she's a junior. What year are you in?

2. My friend was born in China and then grew up in America.

3. Mrs. Zheng, this is a little present which we are giving you.

4. A: How old is her son? B: He's still small. It seems he's seven months old.

5. She's already over 70, but because she eats lots of good things, she looks young.

6. A: Are you married? B: My older brother is already married; I'm not yet married.

7. That Chinese person said that American food looks good but does not taste very good.

8. I have one older sister, she works at Southwest Airlines. Do you have brothers or sisters?

9. Sorry, I forgot to introduce myself. My surname is Huang. I'm a teacher; I teach junior high.

10. A: I suppose your daughter is already in elementary school? B: Yes, she's already in second grade.

Unit 7: Translation Exercise

NAME _____ COURSE _____ DATE _____

Translate the following sentences into Pinyin romanization with correct tone marks. If you have forgotten a word, consult the English-Chinese Glossary in the back of your textbook.

1. Where did you live before coming to America?

2. You say you have one child, right? A boy or a girl? How old?

3. I've heard that Little Chen knows German, French, and Japanese.

4. A: Did you go by yourself? B: No, I went together with three classmates.

5. A: Can you write Chinese? B: I can write a little, but I don't write it very well.

6. Do you know if that American teacher can speak Standard Chinese (Mandarin)?

7. She lived in Spain for over eleven years. No wonder she speaks Spanish so well.

8. After graduating from high school, she worked for two years, then she applied to college.

9. The Chinese University of Hong Kong has several thousand students. Some I know, others I don't.

10. A: You speak English very well, you know! Where did you learn it? B: I learned it in kindergarten.

Unit 8: Translation Exercise

NAME _____ COURSE _____ DATE _____

Translate the following sentences into Pinyin romanization with correct tone marks. If you have forgotten a word, consult the English-Chinese Glossary in the back of your textbook.

1. Excuse me, how do I get to Taiwan University?

2. We'll come looking for you in half an hour, O.K.?

3. It seems that my home is not very far from your home.

4. Miss Li is not at her desk. Please call her again in ten minutes.

5. The tourists who come from America almost all stay at the Beijing Hotel.

6. These two pieces of luggage are mine, those three pieces of luggage are his.

7. Don't get excited, I think Professor Wang is likely to come in just a little while.

8. Keep going straight, after you've passed the French Embassy you then will have arrived.

9. A: How long does it take to get from there to the Foreign Ministry? B: One hour, more or less.

10. Darn it, I forgot! New Asia Trading Co. is closed today. We have no choice but to come again tomorrow.

Unit 9: Translation Exercise

NAME _____ COURSE _____ DATE _____

Translate the following sentences into Pinyin romanization with correct tone marks. If you have forgotten a word, consult the English-Chinese Glossary in the back of your textbook.

1. He's not only stupid but also lazy.

2. First take the bus, then take the trolley.

3. When we get to Tiananmen, please call me.

4. She likes red and blue. What colors do you like?

5. I can't fall asleep on trains. Can you fall asleep on trains?

6. Go straight from here and turn left at the first traffic light.

7. You don't need to ask her, she's not very clear about it either.

8. First turn to the east, then turn to the west, and you'll be there!

9. I'm sorry, I can't find my name cards. (don't use **kéyi** or **néng**)

10. At home we raise fish. Do you keep any small animals at home?

. . . .

Unit 10: Translation Exercise

NAME_____ COURSE _____ DATE _____

Translate the following sentences into Pinyin romanization with correct tone marks. If you have forgotten a word, consult the English-Chinese Glossary in the back of your textbook.

1. When Old Wang died, everybody was very sad.

2. The east coast of the U.S. is not as dry as the west coast.

3. This winter I'm going to Beijing. Is Beijing colder than New York?

4. I'm playing with my computer; Old Sun is sleeping. What are you doing?

5. Macao is hot every day—both hot and humid, so we seldom go outdoors.

6. Recently the weather has been cooler and cooler, more and more comfortable.

7. Starting tomorrow, I'm going to be working at the embassy. I'm so nervous I'm going to die.

8. The weather forecast said that tomorrow the high temperature will be 33° and the low temperature 25°.

9. If it rains tomorrow, then we won't go out to have fun; but the weather report isn't necessarily accurate.

10. A: My friends are neither many nor few. B: I have only one good friend. C: I don't have friends at all.

Praise for the
BASIC MANDARIN CHINESE and
INTERMEDIATE MANDARIN CHINESE textbooks:

"Meticulously planned, carefully prepared and patiently tested for over a decade, the Basic Chinese series represents the most comprehensive introductory materials available now. The eclectic approach, the flexibility in use, the attention to authenticity of language in its sociolinguistic context, the myriad of audio and visual aids, and the array of rigorously designed exercises makes the Basic Chinese the ideal material for any committed learner embarking on the journey of learning the Chinese language."
—Dr. Jun Yang, Senior Lecturer in Chinese, University of Chicago

"Outstanding for its carefully graduated presentation of material ... and perhaps most important of all, its separation of the task of learning to speak the language from the very different processes of learning to read and write Chinese characters ... The most exciting Chinese language textbook I have seen in many years."
—Dr. James E. Dew, retired associate professor of Chinese, Univ. of Michigan; former Director of the Inter-University Program for Chinese Language Studies in Taipei

"Revolutionary in its approach ... The dream of having engaged and fully-prepared students in every class is an easily reachable reality for any program that adopts this series."
—Professor Cecilia Chang, Department of Asian Studies, Williams College

"This is one of the best elementary Chinese textbooks, I believe, ever produced in the history of teaching Chinese as a second language ... A great and unique work which will benefit students and teachers for many years to come."
—Dr. Shengli Feng, Professor of Chinese Linguistics, Chinese University of Hong Kong

"A breath of fresh air... Its dual track for spoken and written language finally gives American students a chance to develop oral proficiency without being slowed down by the character writing... An ideal textbook for any program that seeks to advance rapidly in spoken Chinese and to fully prepare the students for their encounter with China."
—Dr. Jingqi Fu, Associate Professor of Chinese, St. Mary's College of Maryland

"Contextualized so learners know not only what to say, but why, when, and with whom it is appropriate to use such language. ...thorough and clear...refreshing."
—Dr. Matthew Christensen, Professor of Chinese, Brigham Young University

Cornelius C. Kubler is Stanfield Professor of Asian Studies at Williams College, where he teaches Chinese and for many years chaired the Department of Asian Studies. He was formerly Chinese Language Training Supervisor and Chair of the Department of Asian and African Languages at the Foreign Service Institute, U.S. Department of State, where he trained American diplomats in Chinese and other languages, and he served for six years as Principal of the American Institute in Taiwan Chinese Language & Area Studies School. Kubler, who has directed intensive Chinese language training programs in the U.S., mainland China, and Taiwan, has been active in Chinese language test development and has authored or coauthored 20 books and over 50 articles on Chinese language pedagogy and linguistics. He has just completed a two-year tour as American Co-Director of the Johns Hopkins University–Nanjing University Center for Chinese & American Studies in Nanjing, China.

Yang Wang, native to Beijing, is Senior Lecturer in Chinese at Brown University, where she teaches all levels of modern Chinese language. Before joining the Brown faculty, she taught Chinese at The Ohio State University and Williams College. She also taught for several years at the Middlebury College Summer Chinese School. Wang is interested in the implications of pragmatics in Chinese pedagogical practice, teaching materials development, and the integration of technology into the curriculum.